Walking the BLACKDOWNS

Michael G. Harding

HALSGROVE

First published in Great Britain in 1997

British Library Cataloguing-in-Publication Date
A CIP record for this title is available from the British Library

ISBN 1 874448 06 X

HALSGROVE
PUBLISHING, MEDIA AND DISTRIBUTION

Halsgrove House
Lower Moor Way
Tiverton, Devon EX16 6SS
Tel: 01884 243242
Fax: 01884 243325

The mapwork in this book has been drawn by the author with no direct reference to existing mapping. It is recommended, though not essential, that an appropriate OS map is used in conjunction with these walks as suggested on the first page of each walk. All the OS maps referred to are available from Halsgrove at the address above.

Printed and bound in Great Britain by The Devonshire Press, Torquay.

CONTENTS

LIST OF WALKS

LOCATION OF WALKS

USING THIS BOOK

Explanation of instructions given in this book
when passing from field to field

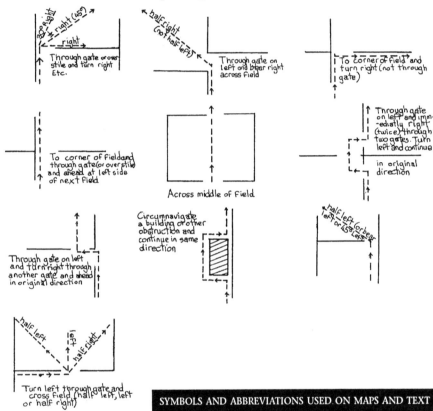

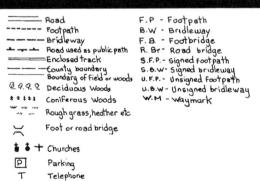

SYMBOLS AND ABBREVIATIONS USED ON MAPS AND TEXT

Symbol	Meaning	Abbreviation	Meaning
———	Road	F.P	Footpath
- - - -	Footpath	B.W	Bridleway
— — —	Bridleway	F.B.	Footbridge
⊥·—·⊥·—	Road used as public path	R. Br	Road bridge
═══	Enclosed track	S.F.P.	Signed footpath
————	County boundary	S.B.W.	Signed bridleway
————	Boundary of field or woods	U.F.P.	Unsigned footpath
℺℺℺℺	Deciduous Woods	U.B.W.	Unsigned bridleway
⚹⚹⚹⚹	Coniferous Woods	W.M.	Waymark
⸺ ⸺	Rough grass, heather etc		
⤳	Foot or road bridge		
⚶ ⚶ ✝	Churches		
Ⓟ	Parking		
T	Telephone		

INTRODUCTION

The idea of a book of walks on the Blackdown Hills has come about threefold. Firstly, I have lived and worked as a farmer on the Hills for 20 years and so have come to love and appreciate the beauty of the area. Secondly, as a diversification from my farming, I have, for a number of years, taken holiday guests staying at my farmhouse out on guided walks. Thirdly, since retiring from farming, I have carried out a survey of all 551 Public Rights of Way (P.R.O.W.) on the Blackdowns, on behalf of the Ramblers Association.

This has taken me into some very quiet and remote places on the Hills, where it is quite possible to walk for a day and hardly meet anyone other than perhaps a working farmer, even on a public holiday. It is this peace and quiet that will appeal to walkers.

As a result of my survey, the idea was born to give others the pleasures of this tranquil rural scene by putting together a representative selection of 20 walks covering the variable scenery of the Blackdowns.

The Blackdown Hills have been designated an Area of Outstanding Natural Beauty (A.O.N.B.) and an environmentally sensitive area (E.S.A.). The area consists of steep, wooded, north facing escarpments, with plateaus deeply dissected by valleys and coombes. The plateaus may be wide and windswept while in the valleys nestle villages and hamlets. An important feature of the Blackdowns is the intricate pattern of small enclosed fields and high hedged lanes.

The area is located south of a line between Taunton, Wellington and the M5. It extends to Culmstock in the west, Honiton and near Axminster to the south, and near Chard in the east (see page 5).

The physical character of the area is dominated by the underlying geology. The area is an outcrop of upper greensand. This is mainly non-calcareous and contains cherts. This is covered by a thin layer of clay with flints and cherts.

Where the greensand meets the underlying impermeable rocks around the edges of ridges, there are spring lines. The sources of several rivers are found here. The rivers Culm, Otter and Yarty flow south and tributaries of the Tone and Fivehead flow northwards. For a deeper understanding of the landscape of the area, a publication by the Countryside Commission called 'The Blackdown Hills Landscape' is useful.

The area of the Blackdowns, covers some 39 parishes (see page 9). Twenty four of these are in the county of Devon and fifteen are in Somerset. The 551 footpaths and bridleways walked in my survey, cover some 340 kilometres. As all the walks are circular it is inevitable that some road and lane walking is necessary to link the paths, but this has been kept to the minimum.

You will notice from the texts that I have mentioned the numbers given to all P.R.O.W. by the parish councils in which they occur.

It is the intention of the Countryside Commission that all P.R.O.W. should be signed, waymarked and walkable by the year 2000. To this end the relevant authorities of Devon and Somerset are working.

Should you find any problems existing still on my walks, it is recommended that you report them to the footpath officers at the Ramblers Association and the County or District Authorities. It will be helpful to them if you quote the reference number of the path, the problem and a map reference. It is important to quote the name of the parish, as the same number will occur in different parishes.

The walks vary in length from 7-10 miles and are within the capability of most able bodied people, and will take between 3-5 hours, plus lunch or tea stops. They are not recommended for young children. Should you take your dog, as I always do, please keep it under control at all times and remember the Country Code and respect those who work and earn their living from the land.

All instructions for moving from field to field are given as you face a gate and pass through it (see page 6 for a few examples).

I hope you will enjoy these walks as much as I have preparing them; and you will appreciate why the Blackdown Hills have been designated an A.O.N.B. and E.S.A.

Michael G. Harding
Exmouth 1997

PARISHES OF THE BLACKDOWNS

Twenty-four Devon Parishes

PARISH	DISTRICT AUTHORITY
Awliscombe	(E.D.)
Axminster	(E.D.)
Broadhembury	(E.D.)
Chardstock	(E.D.)
Clayhidon	(M.D.)
Combe Raleigh	(E.D.)
Cotleigh	(E.D.)
Culmstock	(M.D.)
Dalwood	(E.D.)
Dunkeswell	(E.D.)
Hemyock	(M.D.)
Honiton	(E.D.)
Kentisbeare	(M.D.)
Luppitt	(E.D.)
Kilmington	(E.D.)
Membury	(E.D.)
Monkton	(E.D.)
Payhembury	(E.D.)
Sheldon	(E.D.)
Shute	(E.D.)
Stockland	(E.D.)
Uffculme	(M.D.)
Upottery	(E.D.)
Yarcombe	(E.D.)

Fifteen Somerset Parishes

PARISH	DISTRICT AUTHORITY
Bickenhall	(T.D.)
Buckland St Mary	(S.S.D.C.)
Churchstanton	(T.D.)
Combe St Nicholas	(S.S.D.C.)
Corfe	(T.D.)
Curland	(T.D.)
Orchard Portman	(T.D.)
Otterford	(T.D.)
Pitminster	(T.D.)
Sampford Arundel	(T.D.)
Staple Fitzpaine	(T.D.)
Wambrook	(S.S.D.C.)
Wellington Without	(T.D.)
West Buckland	T.D.)
Whitestaunton	(S.S.D.C.)

Abbreviations

E.D. – East Devon
M.D. – Mid Devon
T.D. – Taunton Deane
S.S.D.C. – South Somerset District Council

Addresses

E.D. – The Knowle, Sidmouth, Devon (01392) 577046

M.D. – Ailsa House, Tidcombe Lane, Tiverton, Devon (01884) 255255

T.D. – The Deane House, Belvedere Road, Taunton, Somerset (01823) 356356

S.S.D.C. – Brympton Way, Yeovil, Somerset (01935) 462462

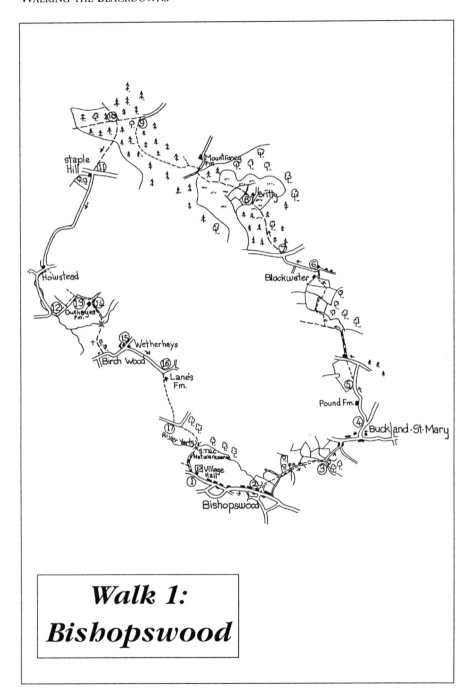

Walk 1: Bishopswood

Walk 1: Bishopswood

BUCKLAND ST MARY • BIRCHWOOD

Start: Village Hall, Bishopswood.
Map ref: ST253128
Distance: 10 miles
Refreshments: Provide your own, Candlelight Inn is at point (2)
Grading: Moderate, but wet in places with some bog
OS Maps: 1:50 000 Landranger - 193 (Taunton and Lyme Regis);
1:25 000 Pathfinder - ST21/31 (1278) Ilminster

DIRECTIONS

(1) Turn left on road from village hall car park to junction. Turn left down through village to the Candlelight Inn.

(2) Turn left on signed F.P. (Buckland St Mary CH3/42) through car park and cross footbridge over River Yarty. Cross field to gate, through and bear half right (waymarked) on F.P. (Buckland St Mary CH3/40, part of) across field to fence in corner. Over this and a crossing track, and down an enclosed track opposite. This narrows to an open and muddy track and descends through woods to cross a footbridge over River Yarty. Keep ahead on footpath, crossing a small stream in two places. Follow a clear track past a cottage to a gate. Make your way ahead on footpath, and through wooded area by a stream to a small waterfall. Cross over a bridge and through a gate on enclosed path to a mill cottage.

(3) Turn left on drive and follow uphill to a road junction. Turn left on road to another junction and right (signed to Buckland St Mary and Chard) to the village and Post Office.

(4) Bear left past the village school, with the church on your right. Turn left at road junction and along Pound Lane, past council houses on your right and Pound Farm on the left. After passing the farm, continue round bends to take the second gate on the left.

(5) Cross field on F.P. (Buckland St Mary CH3/2) towards a thatched cottage and go through gate. Cross road to continue on the same

The Candlelight Inn, Bishopswood

footpath now classified as a bridleway (signed to Blindmoor). Continue down this enclosed track to a gate. Pass through and down an open track to a gate. Keep on the bridleway across a field and over a bridged stream. In a few yards, leave the main track and fork half right on an unsigned F.P. (Still Buckland St Mary CH3/2) and go across a field to find a stile in corner. Over and follow left edge of field to top corner and gate. Through and cross field to small gate. Through and bear left up through two horse paddocks to gate near stables. Through and turn right to stile by gate. Over and keep along left side of field to gate. Follow along an enclosed track to a gate and stile.

(6) Climb over and turn left on a road, past Myrtle Cottage. Avoid a footpath to the right (CH3/1 and signed to Castle Neroche) and continue on the road passing a left junction (signed Blindmoor), to a T junction. Cross straight over this busy road.

(7) Through gate on signed B.W. (Staple Fitzpaine T23/28), Mount Fancy Farm ¾ mile). Follow this forest track, passing a waymarked track to the right. The path becomes boggy, with running water, as it continues to a gate and stile where path turns right. Over this stile and keep on track for 50 yards to the ruins of Britty Farm. Just before these buildings, fork half left into a field, through gateway and cross corner of field to a gap in bank and hedgeline. Cross the next field, slightly left, to find a gap in hedge. Cross a rough field to a gate and stile (waymarked). Over and through bracken and scrubland on clear

bridleway to a gate. Go through and turn right in a few yards to another gate (waymarked). Keep down a track towards Mount Fancy Farm for 50 feet to a gate on the left. (Views to Quantock Hills).

(8) Turn left on F.P. (Staple Fitzpaine T23/26). Follow this clear, but wet track to a waymarked post and fork left on a clear footpath through bracken and into a plantation. There are some very boggy patches on this path. Make your way to a T junction, with forest road, and turn right passing a small cattle shelter and barn on left. Continue to another T junction with a bridleway.

(9) Turn left through gate (waymarked) on this B.W. (Staple Fitzpaine T23/15, part of) and climb uphill through plantation on forest track. Follow past a right junction for 50 yards.

(10) Turn left on B.W. (Staple Fitzpaine T23/16, part of). Ignore gate, stile and B.W. sign on left in 100 yards but proceed up wide track to enter a field in 120 yards. When the right hedge bends to the right, continue straight on across the field to join and follow the line of a wire fence coming in from the left to a gate and very busy road.

(11) Cross over road at junction and down the road opposite. Keep on this road, crossing the infant River Yarty twice, to a T junction. Turn right, and down past a right junction. Follow the River Yarty along the road, crossing it twice again, until the road bends right uphill.

(12) Just before the bend, turn left through gate on signed F.P. (Buckland St Mary 3/14, part of) and climb steeply uphill at right side of field to a gate in top corner. Proceed through the next field to the second gate on the right.

(13) Turn right on clear track (Buckland St Mary CH3/15, part of) at side of field to gate and on down track to second gate (waymarked).

(14) Pass through and turn right on B.W. (B St M CH3/11, part of) to Owlhayes Farm. Enter the farmyard and turn left down bridleway at side of farmhouse. Proceed through gate and down clear track to find gate at bottom. Bear right to cross a footbridge at a ford and follow bridleway up across field and into woods. Emerge again into a field and bear left past a church, to gate, road and B.W. sign at Birchwood.

(15) Turn left on road for half a mile, forking right at Wetherhays Farm, to Lanes Farm.

(16) Turn right up drive to Lanes Farm on F.P. (Buckland St Mary CH3/8), past the farmhouse and through gate to field. Proceed ahead across corner of field to gate. Through, then half left across field to gateway opposite. Keep near right side of field to a small gate.

(17) Turn left on road and at bend in 50 yards, bear right on F.P. (Buckland St Mary CH 3/46) and left in a few yards on track. Follow this enclosed track into a field and cross to another gate and on down to footbridge over River Yarty. Continue on F.P. (Otterford T20/5) bearing right uphill through a nature reserve on a track that follows a hedge to a gate and stile. Keep ahead on enclosed track to a road. Turn left to village hall car park or to the Candlelight Inn.

POINTS OF INTEREST

Buckland St Mary church, built in 1863 by Benjamin Ferry, replacing the 15th century church.

Staple Hill: highest point on the Blackdown Hills (315 metres, 1023 feet).

Bishopswood Meadow Nature Reserve. This reserve is managed by Somerset Wildlife Trust (S.W.T.). It is a fine example of unimproved grassland, resulting in an abundance of wild flowers, grasses and butterflies. The River Yarty runs through the reserve, and kingfishers may be seen. Salmon also come up river to spawn here.

Lime kiln: at the far end of the S.W.T. reserve and is well preserved.

The lime kiln

Walk 2: Castle Neroche

BLACKWATER • CALLOWS FARM • STREET ASH • HAM •
SILVER STREET • HARE • HISBEERS FARM

Start: Forestry Commission Car Park, Castle Neroche
Map ref: ST273157
Distance: 8 miles
Grading: Moderate, steep in places
Refreshments: Eagle Tavern and Ham Hill Garage cafe (on A303)
O.S. Maps: 1:50 000 Landranger - 193 Taunton/Lyme Regis
1:25 000 Pathfinder - ST21/31 (1278) Ilminster

DIRECTIONS

(1) Follow track from car park, in direction of entry, to Castle Neroche Farm on B.W. (Staple Fitzpaine T23/25). Go through gate and a very muddy farmyard. Pass the farmhouse and out on farm drive (Staple Fitzpaine T23/20) to road. Turn left, and in a few yards, turn right on signed F.P. (Buckland St Mary CH3/1). Halfway down this drive, turn right over a stile and then left in field to follow in previous direction to a stile in corner. Then down the left side of second field to a stile. Over and across middle of third field to stile and F.P. sign (former hedgeline removed).

(2) Turn left on road to a left bend by a cottage. Here turn right over a stile in fence beside a drive on F.P. (Buckland St Mary CH3/2) and along an enclosed track to a gate in 50 yards. Through and turn right to a stile. Over and bear left to gate. Proceed straight down a horse paddock to gate and stile. Over and bear right to a small gate. Through and cross field to a gate. Follow the right edge of next field to a stile near corner. Then cross field, bearing half right to a track (B.W.). Turn left and over a field bridge. Continue uphill on this B.W. (still part of CH3/2) to a gate. Through and up left side of field to gate. Follow an enclosed track to road and F.P. sign and turn left.

(3) Just past a bungalow, turn left on B.W. (Buckland St Mary CH3/3). Keep along left side of paddock to a gate on your left. Continue on B.W. track at edge of woods and a rough area to far corner. Turn left

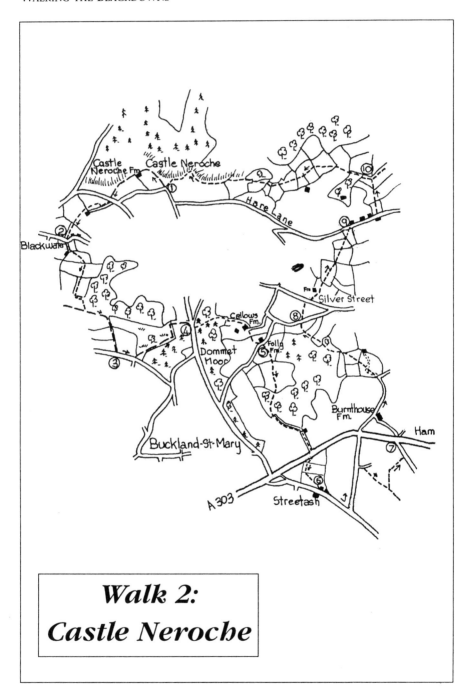

Walk 2:
Castle Neroche

towards farm buildings. Turn right by these on a bank between fences to end of buildings. Turn right on farm drive and continue to a road. Turn right on this very busy road and in a few yards go past a left junction. Cross road (with care) and go through a gap in bank. Now turn right and follow a track running parallel to the road for 150 yards. **(4)** Turn back hard left on clear track (Buckland St Mary CH3/18) to a crossing track. Turn left on this to waymark post. Turn right here and follow waymarks down to corner of plantation at fence (Marvellous views over Vale of Taunton to Quantock Hills). Proceed down field to gate by Callows Farm. Through and down concreted track past farmhouse on right and garage on left. A few yards past the end of post and rail fence, turn right over stile. Cross a wet field to stream. Cross this via steps and stile into field. Bear half left across field to gate and stile onto road at Folly Farm. Turn left on road to double gates on right, in a few yards.

(5) Go through gates (still on Buckland St Mary CH3/18) and climb up across field to the left of island of brambles etc. to gate and stile. Over and straight ahead along removed hedge line (trees remaining), across field and enter woods over stile. Ahead on footpath through woods to main crossing track. Cross straight over and bear left across small corner of trees for 50-60 feet to stile in wire fence. Enter field and follow up left side of this rough field to gate. Through and ahead to stile in paddock fence. Over and turn left. In a few yards, turn right on drive past 'Old Manor'. Turn left at T junction in 100 yards. In 20 yards, turn right and follow drive to A303. Cross straight over to stile in hedge. Over and continue (still on F.P. Buckland St Mary CH3/18) bearing right, 30° from hedge, to gate. Cross second field to gate. Through and turn half left across a third field to gate and road at F.P. sign.

(6) Turn left on this very busy road, past Street Ash Nursery. Turn left at next road junction. In 400 yards, turn right on cart track (Combe St Nicholas CH7/4O part of). In 50 yards, ahead through two gates and along right side of field (fine views). Near end of field, fork left to corner and turn left on F.P. (Combe St Nicholas CH7/41) to follow with hedge on right. At bend in hedge, fork right, across corner of field to gate. Turn right and pass down field to gate. Continue, on enclosed track for 50 yards to join a road at a small gate. Turn left on road to junction with A303.

(7) Cross straight over to minor road (left to Eagle Tavern Inn or right to garage and cafe) and take left fork to Burnt House Farm. Continue past farm to T junction. Turn right and road continues as a F.P. (Combe St Nicholas CH7/39), but deteriorates to a surfaced track. This bends left and then right downhill. Just before a cattle grid, turn left over a stile and into field. Go half right across field (between two gas markers) to a stile in hedge. Over and half right down and across field to gate in corner. Through and turn left to small gate in 40 yards. Enter woods and walk slightly left down through very wet woods (boggy in places) to a gate and stream in corner. Cross and straight ahead on F.P. (Buckland St Mary CH3/25) to a stile. Over and bear slightly left across to a small gate. Through and over stream. Ahead with hedge on your right to a small gate. Pass through and continue in previous direction to a stile and onto road.

(8) Turn left on road and in 20 yards, turn right over stile on F.P. (Buckland St Mary CH3/34). Cross a small stream and walk up and across field to a gate, onto a road. Turn right and in 50 yards, turn left on F.P. (Buckland St Mary CH3/26) to Lane Farm. Continue down this surfaced track to farm. Pass over a piped stream. Climb up across field to a stile in the top right corner. Over and slightly right across two fields (crossing old removed hedge line) to a stile in right hedge, near top corner. Over and across corner of field to stile and steps onto road.

(9) Turn right on road (passing a farm) for 300 yards. Turn left on signed F.P. (Buckland St Mary CH3/28) opposite Braeside. Follow down the right side of field to a stile. Over and at next stile in corner, proceed through a strip of woodland. Leave via a stile into a field. Continue across field to a stile and gate leading onto an enclosed track.

(10) Turn left on F.P. (Buckland St Mary CH3/30, part of). When this ends, turn left over a stile and up the right side of field, by a ditch. Bear right with hedge and ditch to a gateway on right. Through and ahead across field to a stile and F.B. and a second stile. Go across field to gate. Through and turn left across field to gate by barn and stile.

Over and ahead on F.P. (Buckland St Mary CH3/31) and up and across field to gateway. Pass through and continue to another stile. Over and bear left up the 'spine' of the hill to a gate and stile in right corner.

(11) Over and bear left uphill on F.P. (Buckland St Mary CH3/35) to top corner of field. Over stile and another in 50 yards. Turn right in field to stile and left to another stile in 40 feet. Turn by beech trees to stile. Then turn left on part of a 'forest trail', back to your car, following red waymarks.

POINTS OF INTEREST

Castle Neroche: this prehistoric hill fort is 870 feet above sea level. There are fine views across the Vale of Taunton to the Quantock Hills, and across Sedgemoor. William the Conqueror gave the fort to his half brother and the old earthworks were turned into a Norman stronghold. Neroche was once a royal forest, but deforestation was begun in the 1620s by Charles I.

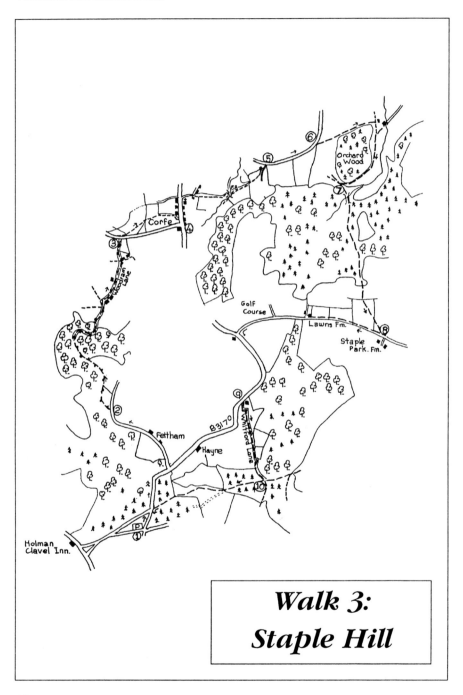

**Walk 3:
Staple Hill**

Walk 3: Staple Hill

FELTHAM • ADCOMBE WOOD • WOODRAM LANE • CORFE • HEALE • STAPLE LAWNS • WHITFORD LANE

Start: Forestry Commission car park on Staple Hill (B3170)
Map ref: ST229162 OR Corfe Church (not on a Sunday)
Distance: 10 miles
Grading: Moderate, steep in places
Refreshments: White Hart Inn, Corfe
O.S. Maps: 1:50 000 Landranger - 193 (Taunton and Lyme Regis)
1:25 000 Pathfinder - 1278 (Ilminster) ST21/31

DIRECTIONS

(1) From car park, turn left to B3170 at crossroads. Turn left downhill past a junction (to Wellington and Churchinford). Continue downhill on this busy road (so take care), to turn left at a junction (signed to Feltham). In half a mile, turn left on signed B.W. (Pitminster T21/84).

(2) Go through a small gate into Adcombe Wood and follow a clear path at edge of woods, avoiding first track to left. After half a mile, the path descends with woods either side. Further down, as the track leaves the woods, it is very wet and is now enclosed by hedges, with fields on both sides. Go past Higher Woodram Farm and bear right to follow this now metalled road past Middle Woodram Farm and Lower Woodram Farm, to a T junction in half a mile.

(3) Turn left and in 30 yards, turn right over stile on signed F.P. (Pitminster T21/24). Turn right in field to follow parallel with the road to a corner. Cross over a stile and F.B. into field. Follow the headland around corner of field to just past a pond. Turn right through gap in wire fence on F.P. (Corfe T8/10) into next field. Then cross this on an unploughed F.P. to join the hedge line. Bear right with this and over a stile, towards the end of the field to a gate. Emerge onto a road (B3170) at F.P. sign in Corfe.

(4) Cross this very busy road, and turn left to use the footway. Continue through the village and turn right into Mill Lane (opposite a telephone box) on F.P. (Corfe T8/4). Go past the Church of St Nicholas

(N.B. parking available by church if starting from Corfe). Make your way along to a bungalow called 'Broad Ridge' on the left. Pass to the right of this on a walled track to a left bend and F.P. sign, by a garage. Keep forward and follow at the left side of a field to a kissing gate on your left. Through and proceed in previous direction, now at the right side of a field, by a deep ravine to a F.B. Over this and a stile, to turn left in a field, on signed F.P. (Corfe T8/3, part of) to gate in corner. Through and head to a gate by Home Meadow Cottage.

(5) Pick up a road to a T junction by Heale House and turn right for nearly half a mile to a right turning near 'Mill House'.

(6) Just past this junction, turn through a small gate on right and cross a field (often with a crop in it), half left on B.W. (Orchard Portman T19/6) to corner of Orchard Wood. Pass into next field and follow right edge of field by woods on a headland. Orchard Portman church is seen away to the left and also Taunton racecourse, with the Quantock Hills beyond. When the woods end, turn right through a gate in 50 yards on unsigned F.P. (Orchard Portman T19/10) just before a cottage. Cross a paddock, slightly left on a track parallel to woods, to join a surfaced track. Turn right on this fenced B.W. and ahead to a gate. Through and fork left (avoiding right fork into forest). Head up the valley with woods to your right. Track becomes enclosed and bears right. Continue to a crossing track.

(7) Turn left on this B.W. (Staple Fitzpaine T23/19, part of) and pass through a small gate, before continuing on a clear track in woods. Pass over a deep ravine, and continue to a main 'forestry' road at a bend. Go forward uphill for quarter of a mile on this track, until it bends back to the left. Now leave main track and head forward on unsigned B.W. uphill. When this ends at a gate, cross a field at left edge to another gate. Proceed half left across a large field to Staple Park Farm.

(8) Do not go through small gate to farm, but turn right on another signed B.W. (Staple Fitzpaine T23/18). Keep to the left side of two large fields to Lawns Farm. Pass through a small gate towards a wooden bungalow. Turn left for 50 yards. Then right onto a track that becomes a surfaced road, passing a private road to golf course. Continue to a T junction with B3170.

(9) Turn left up Whitford Hill for half a mile to a property called Lower Hayne. Just past this, turn left on drive to Whitford Hayne (B.W. Staple Fitzpaine T23/16, part of). Turn right just short of entrance gates and cattle grid, through a small gate up Whitford Lane. Climb this signed B.W. uphill on clear track for half a mile to a T junction with another forest road.

(10) Turn right uphill on this B.W. (Staple Fitzpaine T23/15, part of), past a left junction in 50 yards. Continue to climb through forest to a gate into a field. Leave the surfaced track here and fork right, as the B.W. follows the right hedge to a gate. Ahead through gorse, bracken and birch on a clear track to a waymark post. Keep forward (do not enter plantation yet) to a small gate. Enter the plantation on a track to road (B3170 again), opposite road junction. Turn left to crossroads in 200 yards and turn right to car park and picnic area.

POINTS OF INTEREST

Holman Clavel Inn (near the start) is 600 years old and used to be a coaching house for monks travelling from Exeter to Glastonbury.

The beam across the chimney is of holly. *Holm* means holly and *clavel* means chimney beam. Hence the name Holman Clavel Inn. The pub is said to be haunted by a ghost called Charlie, who it is alleged was once a monk. For doing something 'naughty', he was defrocked, and probably took his own life. Good refreshments may be obtained here if this walk was started at Corfe.

Hayne: this was a royal lodge.

Corfe is a pretty village on the northern slopes of the Blackdowns, four miles from Taunton on the B3170. The name is derived from an ancient name meaning gap or pass, and the Honiton road goes through this.

Lime was quarried and kilned for agricultural use. The ancient woodland, which used to provide fuel for the kilns, still exists. The village has won the 'Best Kept Small Village' competition in Somerset on several occasions.

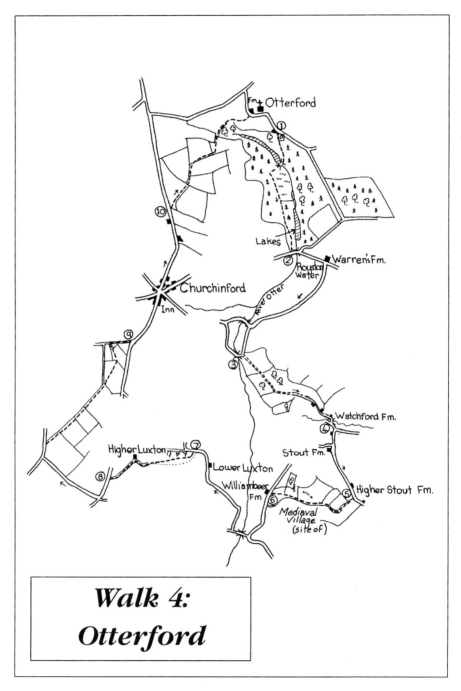

**Walk 4:
Otterford**

Walk 4: Otterford

Royston Water • Watchford Farm •
Medieval Village • Luxton • Churchinford

Start: Wessex Water Board car park, Otterford Lake
Map ref: ST 224142
Distance: 8 miles
Grading: Moderate
Refreshments: Provide your own
O.S. Maps: 1:50 000 Landranger - 193 (Taunton)
1:25 000 Pathfinder - ST21/31 (1278) Ilminster

DIRECTIONS

(1) From car park, descend on F.P. (Otterford T20/15) by notice board. In 30 yards go down steps and turn left on track to lake. Cross bridge and turn left to gate and stile on left in 30 yards. Over stile and through rough field to enter plantation by stile. Follow path through plantation, soon joining part of Churchstanton T6/23. Continue on this track avoiding nature trail on left and down muddy track to road.

(2) Turn left past Royston Water and past a left junction. Climb uphill, and turn right opposite Warrens Farm. Follow along lane for half a mile and down to cottage. Turn left on road that follows the River Otter.

(3) Turn left through small gate by cattle grid, just before the road crosses the river. Follow this pretty unfenced road for half a mile to Watchford Farm. Bear right by farm and through small gate by cattle grid. Continue over bridge and uphill past Stout Mill Cottage on right and road junction on left.

(4) Pass another junction on right at farm. In quarter mile, pass Higher Stout Farm on left.

(5) Just before a cottage on left, turn right on signed F.P. (Yarcombe 16). Over stile and follow down right side of field, passing gate on right. Bend right with hedge and over a bank to follow a track enclosed by a stone wall. Keep on this track which bends about (fine views down Otter Valley) to a gate. Through and ahead on unfenced

track by stone wall. Site of medieval village is now passed on right. Pass a gate on left and through a gateway ahead. Continue with wall still on left. When this bends left, proceed straight ahead down to stile in right hedge. Over and across field towards farm. On reaching corner of field, go over stile and down steps onto road and F.P. sign at Williambeer Farm.

(6) Turn left on road and right at next junction. Cross over River Otter and turn right again. Follow this road uphill past Pamos Farm on left and Lower Luxton Farm on right.

(7) After a left bend, turn left over stile and F.B. on signed F.P. (Upottery 19), and proceed up the left side of woods for 50 yards. Then turn right on a wide track by bank of bracken on left and woods on right. Path opens out as a field. Keep to left side of this narrow field. Leave by gate at far end. Continue on enclosed track, passing a small cattle yard and barn. Pass through a small white gate. The path now leads into part of the garden of Luxton Farm. You then turn left on farm road. Cross a cattle grid and follow to a road.

(8) Turn left and then right at crossroads. Proceed for one third of a mile and turn right in 50 yards on signed F.P. (Churchstanton T6/25). This is enclosed for 100 yards. Through gate and keep to left side of field to stile. Over and along edge of a long field to gate. Proceed half-right across next field to far corner. Over stiles and straight across field to gate leading onto an enclosed track. At junction, turn right to road.

(9) Turn left to Churchinford village. Pass through the village and out past an old chapel on left and village hall on right. Keep on road for half a mile, passing The Lodge on your right and a house and barn on left.

(10) Turn right through gate 100 yards past this house on signed F.P. (Churchstanton T6/20). Follow down right side of field to corner. Go through the right of two gateways and down left side of second field to corner. Over a stile and down third field to gate. Enter fourth field and turn right along fence to gate on right. Here turn left and across to corner of field by woods (N.B. Hedges marked on O.S. map have been removed in this field). Through gate on right in wire fence and bear left across piped ditch. Continue at right side of field by woods.

Through gate on F.P. (Otterford T20/22) and over a ditch. Then cross field in direction of farm. Leave field by gate to the right of these. Turn right on road at Otterford. Pass farm buildings and church on road back to car park.

POINTS OF INTEREST

Otterford Lakes, owned by Wessex Water Authority and leased to Forestry Commission and Somerset Wildlife Trust.

Medieval village, site of, paragraph 5.

Otterford Church - Once used as a pilgrimage church between Exeter and Glastonbury and run by two monks who lived at the Holman Clavel Inn. Two very old table tombs may be found, dating back to 1629, probably the oldest in the Blackdowns.

Churchinford is a village with a six cross centre. Postboys and Ostler Cottage in Moor Lane, both 250 years old. When the postboy rode in with the mail his horse would be attended to by the ostler.

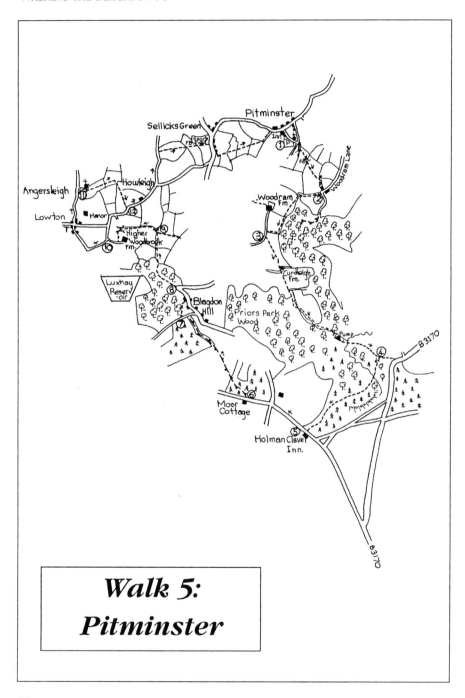

**Walk 5:
Pitminster**

Walk 5: Pitminster

CURDLEIGH • HAWKSMOOR • HOLMAN CLAVEL INN •
BLAGDON HILL • HIGHER WOODBROOK FARM • ANGERSLEIGH •
HOWLEIGH • SELLICKS GREEN

Start: Pitminster Church car park (not during service time)

Map ref: ST220191

Distance: 7½ miles

Grading: Moderate, with some steep climbs

Refreshments: Holman Clavel Inn

O.S. Maps: 1:50 000 Landranger - 193 (Taunton and Lyme Regis)
1:25 000 Pathfinder - ST21/31 (1278) Ilminster ST01/11 (1277)
Culm Valley ST01/11 (1277)

DIRECTIONS

(1) From car park, go through churchyard and out onto a road. Turn right past Chilcotts Farm, to gate and signed F.P. on left (Pitminster T21/66). Through gate and follow at left edge of field to a fence. Climb over and across two F.B.s into second field. Cross this at 30° from the hedge to a F.B. Cross over into third field and bear right across to the right side of an old tin barn. Continue along edge of field to gate and stile. Follow an enclosed track to a junction with signed B.W. (Pitminster T21/84, part of), at Higher Woodram Cottages. Turn right on track for 50 yards to gate.

(2) Turn right through gate on signed B.W. (Pitminster T21/62) and along right edge of field to a F.B. Cross over and ahead to stile and junction with another F.P. (Pitminster T21/61). Climb over and straight ahead to corner of field. Turn right to stile and F.P. sign. Turn left on farm road (Pitminster T21/57, part of). Just before bridge, turn left over a stile on signed F.P. (Pitminster T21/68).

(3) Keep at the right side of a field to a F.B. and fence, leading into a garden. Climb over and follow path between stream and a wall, to a small gate. Now turn right and in a few yards, turn left through a gate. Follow a track in field to gate. Follow this same track up through a plantation for about 200 yards. Fork left on a waymarked path into woods and follow across a stream. Turn right along the stream and

look out for waymarks on trees. Continue through woods to a pumping station. Turn right and then left by the perimeter wire fence and go forward to a stream. Cross over (parish boundary) and F.P. continues uphill as Otterford T20/20 on an enclosed track through woods over Hawkes Moor.

(4) At a right junction, turn right on a wide track (Otterford T20/18) in woods, down to cross a stream. Then climb up steeply in plantation to a crossing forest track. Turn left and in 30 yards, bear right. Path levels out and continues as a wide forest road to a stile and gate in half a mile. Follow onto a road near the Holman Clavel Inn and refreshments.

(5) Turn right on road to a crossroads in 400 yards (take care on this busy road). Cross straight over and on for a further 300 yards to Moor Cottage on the left.

(6) Turn right opposite the cottage on a track (Pitminster T21/79) through an avenue of beech trees for three quarters of a mile. (There are fine views here across the Vale of Taunton, the Somerset Levels and the Quantock Hills). The track descends down to a road. Turn left to a cottage in 120 yards.

(7) Turn right down the far side of the cottage on an unsigned F.P. (Pitminster T21/77, part of) through woods by a stream. The path then bends around the garden of a house to a road. Turn left downhill to a hairpin bend in 200 yards.

(8) From this sharp bend on Blagdon Hill, turn left on signed F.P. (Pitminster T21/53) and follow a clear track through woods. The path tops a rise and turns right on signed F.P. Keep on a clear track (look out for badger sett down through pretty woods. There are waymarks on trees. Further down, the path takes a right and left bend. Then follow a ditch down to enter a field. (There are fine views of Blagdon Village and Pitminster Church spire, Taunton Vale and Adcombe Hill, on your right). Proceed down the left edge of a field by woods to a stile. Then down the side of a second field to another stile on left.

(9) Turn left over the stile on F.P. (Pitminster T21/52, part of). In 50 yards, cross over a stile and turn right to follow a hedgerow down to a F.B. Cross this and turn left to a gate, stile and F.P. sign. Turn right on

the entrance drive from Higher Woodbrook Farm to a junction with a road at a F.P. sign.

(10) Turn left and follow a twisting lane to arrive at a crossroad and cottages, near a telephone box at Angersleigh. Cross straight over and uphill for 400 yards.

(11) Turn right on signed F.P. (Pitminster T21/46) to Angersleigh church. Go past the church on a fenced path to a small gate. Pass through and across parkland in front of Leigh Court to a gate and stile. Cross a second field at the right edge to a small white gate. Turn right and go across a field to a stile and F.B. Cross the next field to the end of a hedgerow. Go past this and across the remainder of the field to a gate and F.P. sign.

(12) Turn left on road for 400 yards to junction at Howleigh. Turn left for 400 yards to signed F.P. (Pitminster T21/50). Turn right over a stile. Proceed down through a large field to a stile and F.B. Cross this and follow the right edge of next field to enter and cross a playing field to a road and F.P. sign at Sellick Green. Turn right for 100 yards to a signed F.P. (Pitminster T21/55) on the opposite side of the road. Turn left over a stile and follow a clear F.P. through several fields, to emerge at a road in Pitminster. Turn right to the pub and right again to the church car park.

POINTS OF INTEREST

Holman Clavel Inn: see walk 3 for details.

Pitminster: the parish of Pitminster, including the hamlets of Blagdon, Leigh Fulford, Trendle, Duddlestone and the village of Pitminster itself, was given to the Church of Winchester by King Hardicanute. In 1351 the Black Death swept through the parish.

The Queens Arms: the oldest part of this pub was once a mill, perhaps the mill recorded for Pitminster in Domesday Book.

Pitminster church (St Mary and St Andrew) was built in the 13th century on the site of a Saxon church, of local greystone. Parts of the nave and the tower are over 700 years old. The tower is unusual and has a normal square base, with an octagonal belfry. The spire is covered in lead. It is said to lean. The pulpit (Jacobean) which is carved, is one of very few with a canopy.

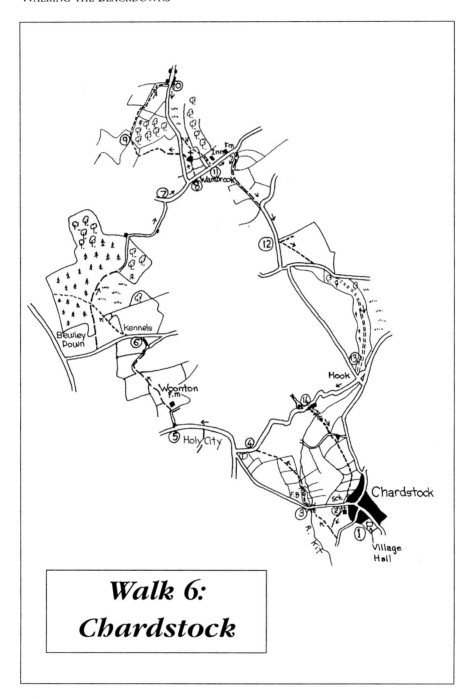

Walk 6: Chardstock

Walk 6: Chardstock

HOLY CITY • WOONTON FARM • BEWLEY DOWN • WAMBROOK

Start: Chardstock village hall car park or Cotley Inn, Wambrook
Map ref: ST311043
Distance: 8 ½ miles
Grading: Moderate.
Refreshments: Cotley Inn, Wambrook or George Inn, Chardstock
O.S. Maps: 1:50 000 Landranger - Taunton and Lyme Regis
1:25 000 Pathfinder - ST20/30 (1297) Chard

DIRECTIONS

(1) Turn left out of Chardstock village hall car park. Go past a junction on your left and the George Inn on right, to the village church.

(2) Turn left on signed F.P. (Chardstock No. 32) through churchyard, passing to the right of the church to a post and rail fence. Turn right for few yards. Then left and right between stone walls to a stile. Here turn left past a conifer plantation. Then cross a small paddock to a gap through into next field. Proceed across middle of field to a stile opposite. Over and turn right on F.P. (Chardstock No. 31) and along hedgeline to gateway. Through and bear half left down across middle of field. Climb over a stile by the River Kit. Continue to a road in 50 yards.

(3) Turn left over River Kit bridge and then right on signed F.P. (Chardstock No. 27). After 30 yards turn right with F.P. and on to cross over two F.B.s. Turn right in field to a stile. Over and turn slightly left across corner of field to gate. Through and across another field, again slightly left and uphill to a stile near top corner. Over and bear left across field to gate near riding school. Cross to second gate and follow drive to road and F.P. sign.

(4) Turn left to a T junction. Then turn right (signed Membury and Chard) for half a mile, passing a number of cottages. Go past a white house on left with a wheel gate and past 'Old Orchard' on the right.

(5) Turn right on unsigned B.W. (Chardstock No. 19) which is the

entrance drive to Woonton Farm. On approaching the farm, bear right with the farm road and then in a few yards, turn left to a small gate. Cross field to a gap in hedge. Through and cross a large field, bearing slightly left, to eventually join the hedgeline. Follow this to end of field. Avoid gate in far corner, but go through gate on right into woods. Follow this muddy B.W. through at edge of a wooded area. Turn left by Sycamore Cottage and continue to road and B.W. sign.

(6) Turn left and in 100 yards, turn right on signed F.P. (Chardstock No. 17) and bear left across a green area (not into kennels) to a drive. Turn right on this footpath, which passes right past the front door and through garden of a cottage to a small gate. Through and past another cottage and turn right on a clear unfenced track through wood and scrubland to a junction with B.W. (Chardstock No. 64). Turn right on this and fork right in 30 yards near plantation. This stony track descends through woods and becomes surfaced. Proceed to a T junction.

(7) Turn right on road and on down past a left junction to a small gate on left.

(8) Unless refreshments are now required at the Cotley Inn, turn left through this small gate and ahead across a foot plank over a small stream. Now walk to Wambrook church. Turn left by church and down to a stile. Over and turn right and just past a phone box, turn left over stile on F.P. (Wambrook No. 25/6, part of). Keep at right side of field to a small gate. Enter woods and follow a clear track to a gate. In a few more yards, turn left on a crossing track and follow for 100 yards to a gate. Enter field and cross to top right corner to a small gate and stile.

(9) Over and turn right to a gate in 50 yards and path continues as F.P. (Wambrook No. 25/5). Keep at the right edge of the next field to a stile in corner. Turn right over this for 50 feet and then turn left along hedgerow. At the end of this field, through a gate and along an enclosed track to a road at Wambrook House.

(10) Turn right on road for ¼ mile to a property called 'Old Smithy'. Turn left over a stile on F.P. (Wambrook No. 25/8). Bear down to the right to follow a stream through two small paddocks. Cross the stream

on F.B. 150 feet before the end of the second paddock and take a path that runs above a bracken slope, besides a wood. Look out for a concealed stile in corner. Go over this and follow an enclosed track to the car park of the Cotley Inn.

(11) Turn left uphill and past Dennetts Farm. Turn right on a signed B.W. (Wambrook 25/4). Climb this stony enclosed track for 200 yards to a crossing gate. Then continue up the right side of two fields to bend in road (B.W. sign). Continue straight ahead and turn left on a signed F.P. through the second of two gates.

(12) Fork half right across a large field to a gate 100 yards from lower corner. Turn left on farm track. Fork right in 150 yards down through a valley on clear track for over half a mile to road.

(13) Go straight ahead over crossroads and follow through Hook for quarter of a mile. Turn left over a stile on signed F.P. (Chardstock 24) just after a pair of redbrick cottages.

(14) Cross down a rough field with bramble patches to a F.B. Climb steeply uphill to a gate in top corner. Cross over a farm track and through a gate. Cross a narrow field to gate. Through and bear left in first field and then across four more fields to gate near the school. Follow track to road and turn left and back through Chardstock to the village hall car park.

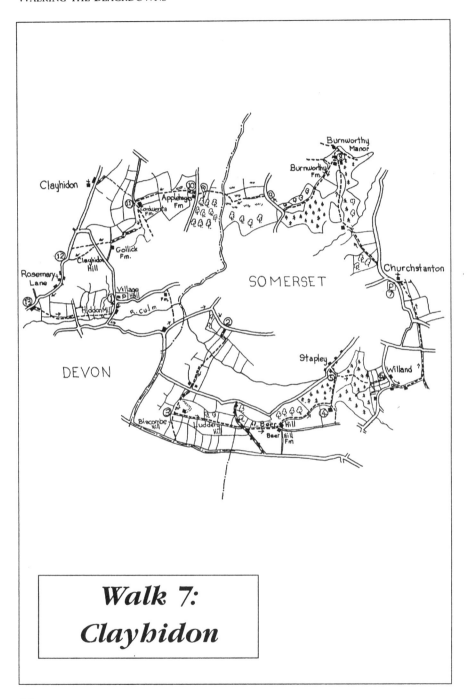

Clayhidon

Burnworthy
Manor

Burnworthy
Fm.

Applehayes
Fm.

Gordwents
Fm.

Gollick
Fm.

Clayhidon
Hill

Churchstanton

SOMERSET

Rosemary
Lane

Village

Hiddon Mill

R. Culm

DEVON

Stapley

Willand

Biscombe
Hill

Luddery
Hill

Beer Hill

Beer Hill
Fm.

Walk 7: Clayhidon

Walk 7: Clayhidon *(Village Hall)*

LILLYCOMBE FARM • BRIMLEY CROSS • BISCOMBE HILL • BEER HILL •
WILLAND • CHURCHSTANTON • BURNWORTHY FARM • APPLEHAYES
FARM • CORDWENTS FARM • ROSEMARY LANE • RIVER CULM

Start: Clayhidon Village Hall - N.B. This is one mile from Clayhidon
Map ref: ST165143
Distance: 9½ miles
Grading: Moderate to strenuous - some wet places
Refreshments: Provide your own
O.S. Maps: 1:50 000 Landranger - 193 (Taunton and Lyme Regis)
1:25 000 Pathfinder - ST01/11, (Culm Valley)

DIRECTIONS

(1) Turn left out of car park and ignore a left turn. Continue down
road past Hiddon Mill (now a residence), and over the River Culm.
Just before a T junction, look out on the right for a plaque in the
hedgebank (see notes at end). Turn left at the junction (signed to
Churchstanton). Proceed along road for 400 yards to road junction at
Lillycombe Farm. Turn left here and ahead over a brook. Continue
uphill to Brimley Farm. Turn right at junction (signed to Brimley and
Churchstanton).

(2) In 400 yards, turn right down enclosed track on signed F.P.
(Churchstanton T6/9) to gate. Do not go through gate but turn left on
enclosed track (very wet) to a stile on right. Over and down field to
stream. Cross by stepping stones. Proceed to top right corner. Cross a
fence and stile on your right and turn left up side of field to gate.
Through and follow track past Biscombe Hill Farm to a road and F.P.
sign in 100 yards. Cross over and through white gates. Follow drive
on signed F.P. (Churchstanton T6/8, part of) toward house. At a left
bend, go straight ahead uphill beside beech trees to enter grounds of
house. Follow the hedge past the level of a white house to near an
enclosed track.

(3) Turn left on unsigned F.P. (Churchstanton T6/7, part of) to cross the
lawn of the house with a hedge on your right (N.B. This is the correct
legal route). Go past the house and lawn and across a large area of

rough grass to woods. Walk through the woods, near to hedge. Divert around fallen trees and enter a field via a stile (W.M.) Cross two fields (passing a farm away to your right) to the narrow end of the second field. Climb over a stile and out onto a lane and F.P. sign. Cross this to a stile opposite and climb over. Now cross a long field by woods to a gate made of barbed wire. Through and circumnavigate to the left of Beerhill Farm to a second wire gate. Cross a farm track and through a third wire gate. Cross an area of grass between woods and farm buildings to a fourth wire fence gate. Go through some nettles and enter woods. Continue through at the right edge, avoiding fallen trees, to a stile. Ahead on clear path towards Pay Farm.

(4) Near the farm, turn left to stile in a corner. Climb over and down steps on F.P. (Churchstanton T6/6). Now walk on a boundary bank in woods. Follow this down to a crossing track. Then ahead to cross a stream. Keep on track for 40 feet to a left bend.

(5) Turn right over a stile on F.P. (Churchstanton T6/5). At the end of a wall, cross over a second stile and a piped stream. Continue through a plantation to a F.B. Cross, and up through an area of cleared plantation. Enter woods and cross a F.B. Then follow F.P. through more cleared plantation. Go over a wide crossing track and straight ahead to a stile and across two small paddocks to another stile (W.M.) Cross a third paddock to a gateway. Cross a fourth field to a stile in top corner on right. Turn right over this and immediately left to gate, stile and F.P. sign, near Higher Willand Farm.

(6) Turn right on road. Then turn left at F.P. sign, on track past a 'Green' at Willand. Follow this enclosed track as F.P. (Churchstanton T6/17) to a T junction. Turn left (still Churchstanton T6/17). Continue on this track to road and F.P. sign. Cross over road and follow another enclosed track as same F.P. to another road and F.P. sign. Cross over to gate and F.P. sign. Follow left edge of field to a stile. Then bear left across middle of next field to a gate near vicarage. Join a track to a road in 50 yards and F.P. sign.

(7) Turn right past Churchstanton church (worth looking inside this church, with its box pews). This is an alternative car park to start the walk from on weekdays only. Turn right at next junction (by an old

pub, now a dwelling). Continue downhill for 150 yards to a stile. Cross over this and a F.B. on signed F.P. (Churchstanton T/61) and walk down the left side of three fields to gateway onto a track to Venn Farm. Follow this to the left and over a vehicle bridge and in 20 yards, fork right by a chicken run (W.M.). Climb steeply uphill through woods (pheasants about, so keep dogs on leads until next road is reached), to a stile. Over and follow right edge of field by woods to a stile. Proceed up the side of a second field to the top, narrow corner, to a gate. Through and across a small paddock to enter woods over a stile. The woods are used for pheasant rearing. Follow a wire enclosure and emerge on a farmtrack to Burnworthy Farm.

(8) Turn right on this track and in 100 feet, turn left between barns. Turn left through gate on unsigned F.P. (Churchstanton T6/12). Follow a track through two fields to a gate. Through and bear left in woods on clear track to gate. Ahead on track through field to gate onto road. Turn right uphill through woods and around a bend. At end of woods, turn left through gate, covered in chain link fencing, on unsigned F.P. (still on Churchstanton T6/12).

(9) In a few yards, turn through gate on right into field. Turn left down to a small gate. Continue down the left side of a rough field, and when wire fence ends, go straight ahead, down through bracken, brambles and gorse etc. on an unclear F.P. Turn right on a crossing track and follow down to stream, gate, stile and F.B. on Somerset Devon border. Cross over and F.P. continues as F.P. (Clayhidon 11) past ponds. Continue on a clear grass path through a deciduous plantation. Keep to the right side. On reaching a corner, climb over a wire fence and plank over a ditch. Cross another plantation and across a ditch and bank. Proceed across a wet and wooded area, up to a stile. Climb over and up a steep field to gate, road and F.P. sign.

(10) Cross over road (still on Clayhidon 11) and past Applehayes Farm on signed F.P. on track to gate. Cross field to a gate. Through and across next field to end of hedge. Now cross field in line of removed hedgerow to a gate. Through and down the right side of a field (usually containing horses). Go out through gate near stables, via a diversion to a road.

(11) Turn left on drive to barn conversions at Cordwents Farm on unsigned F.P. (Clayhidon 8, part of). Go through the conversions to gate, and enter a paddock. Follow the fencing to a stile on the right. Continue down through a wooded area on F.P. (Clayhidon 16) to a stile. Over and turn right. Go down through a very wet wooded area to a wire fence. Follow down an enclosed track and go up to Gollick Park Farm. Cross farm road to gate and across field to a gate in direction of a cottage, to road and F.P. sign. Turn right and in a few yards, turn left on signed F.P. (Clayhidon 19) up the drive of Ashcott. In 50 feet, cross over a stile on signed F.P. Cross a large field over Clayhidon Hill to a gateway, and across field to a gate and short track to a road and F.P. sign.

(12) Turn left and down through Rosemary Lane. Turn right at a T junction (signed to Hemyock and Culmstock). Follow road downhill to a small barn in 400 yards. Go past this for 40 yards to stile. Turn left over this on signed F.P. (Clayhidon 21) down left side of field to stile. Over and bear right across field to gate in corner on the right. Through and turn left by hedge to fence (with River Culm on your right). Over and cross next field to gate. Follow a short track past cottages to a road. Turn right and in a few yards, turn left on signed F.P. (still Clayhidon 21) Go through a gate and across a small and wet field by River Culm to a gate. Cross another field by the river to a stile. Cross a third and fourth field to gate and road, at F.P. sign, by a mill conversion (Hiddon Mill). Turn left back to village hall.

POINTS OF INTEREST.

Commemorative plaque to a murder (see photo). The plaque may be found in the right hedge after crossing the River Culm, near the beginning of the walk and just before a T junction.

Rosemary Lane in Clayhidon parish. The Blackdown Hills Mission was started here in 1863 by George Brealey. Other chapels were to follow at Bolham, Stapley, Bishopswood, Browdan, The Lamb, Sheldon etc. The original chapel at Rosemary Lane is still used.

The artist, Robert Bevan, lived at Applehayes. He was a member of the Camden Town group, which flourished in London early this century.

Hiddon Mill: mentioned in Domesday Book. Still a Hiddon Mill today, but is now a residence. Buried within the walls have been found the original cruck frames, showing that it is one of the oldest houses in the parish.

Churchstanton: there was a large settlement here in ancient times. The village was part of Devon until 1896. The church has high box pews with gates.

Rosemary Lane Chapel. One of the Blackdown Mission chapels.

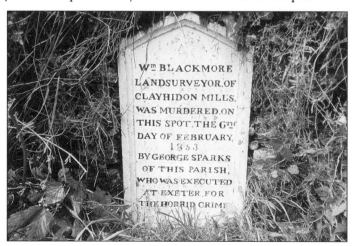

Plaque commemorating the murder of William Blackmore in 1853.

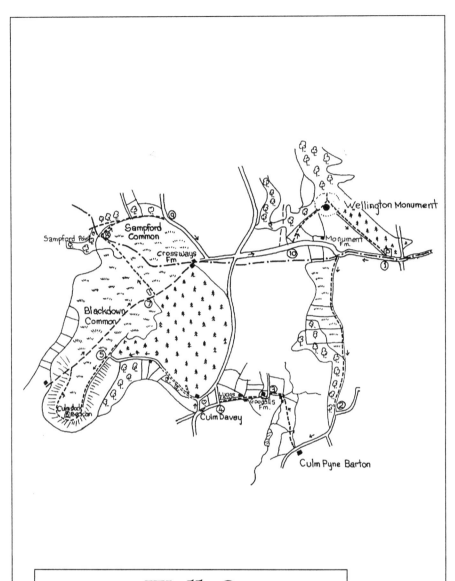

Walk 8:
Wellington Monument

Walk 8: Wellington Monument

CULM PYNE BARTON • CULM DAVY • CULMSTOCK BEACON •
BLACKDOWN COMMON • SAMPFORD COMMON

Start: Monument car park.
Map ref: ST143167
Distance: 7 miles
Grading: Easy
Refreshments: Provide your own
O.S. Maps: 1:50 000 Landranger - 181 (Minehead & Brendon Hills)
1:25 000 Pathfinder - ST01/11 (1277) Culm Valley

DIRECTIONS

(1) From Monument car park, turn right on road for 500 yards. Just before a 'Z' bend turn left over a stile on unsigned F.P. (Hemyock 6). Walk down the right side of field to a stile. Over and ahead on a wide F.P. to stile. Continue through gorse and along left edge of field. Cross another stile and keep on a woodland path at the left edge to a stile. Continue through the next field, passing a summerhouse. This field has a wooded slope to the right. After the next stile, continue on a fenced path to a road and F.P. sign.

(2) Turn right and down a steep hill. Turn right at the next junction. Just past Culm Pyne Barton House, turn right through gate on signed F.P. (Hemyock 13d). Keep at the right edge of field to gate. Go straight across the next field to a gap into a third field. Cross field to a gate near far left corner. Then bear left past farm buildings and uphill on track to gate and F.P. sign.

(3) Turn left past Goodall's Farm. Turn right through gate of farmyard (still on Hemyock F.P. 13d) on signed F.P. Go through the yard and a second gate into a field. In a few yards, turn right through gateway and immediately turn left and follow up the left side of the next field to corner. Cross over a stile and a second stile within a few yards. Keep on grass path to a road. Bear left and ahead past a house, on a private road to cattle grid and small gate, at bend in a road.

(4) Proceed straight ahead on road. Turn right at next junction, by a

letter box on a drive to a cottage. Bear left on reaching the cottage. The drive continues as a track through woods. Fork left at a fork and keep on this clear and wide forest track for ½ mile to a T junction.

(5) Turn left and in a few yards fork left. Continue on a clear path, with good views down to Hemyock and the Culm Valley, for half a mile. When a wire fence bends down to the left, go straight on to Culmstock Beacon.

(6) Turn right at the Beacon on a stony track which follows through bracken, gorse and heather over Blackdown Common. Turn right at a junction with a main B.W. track (Culmstock 34). Continue over the common, avoiding a right junction for three quarters of a mile. The track has become very wide. Bear right near the end to a pond. Turn sharp left just past the pond on a lesser track (Culmstock 35).

(7) This heads roughly in a N.E. direction over Sampford Common towards Sampford Point.

(8) Near the point, avoid a right back turn, but in a few more yards, bear right on a wide and stony track downhill (Sampford Arundel WG 10/7), across Sampford Common (Views to Wellington and across the Quantock Hills). Keep on this track and on reaching a drive on the left, turn right on a signed F.P. to a small gate. Continue in woods (now F.P. Wellington Without WG 13/20) to a road and F.P. sign.

(9) Turn right on road for half a mile to crossroads. Ahead for 400 yards and pass an enclosed track. Go past this for a further 100 yards.

(10) Turn left over a stile on a signed F.P. (Wellington Without WG 13/17). Climb up, slightly left to join a hedgeline at a F.P. sign. Continue in direction of the monument to a stile. Over and ahead to another stile, gate and F.P. sign. Proceed to Wellington Monument in 100 yards.

(11) Leave the monument and return to the entrance car park in half a mile on F.P. (Wellington Without WG 13.22)

POINTS OF INTEREST

Wellington Monument: (see notice board for more details) was erected to the first Duke of Wellington and work was completed in 1892. The monument is 175 feet high. It is floodlit at night and can be seen for miles around by day and night. The monument can be climbed and access obtained by collecting a key. In 1989, restoration work was carried out. The woodland below is owned by the National Trust. The meadows below are managed by Somerset Wildlife Trust.

Culmstock Beacon: there is an interesting stone hut on the Beacon. The latter was lit to warn of the approach of the Spanish Armada. Wellington Monument can be seen from the Beacon and this walk links the two via Blackdown Common.

The Wellington Monument

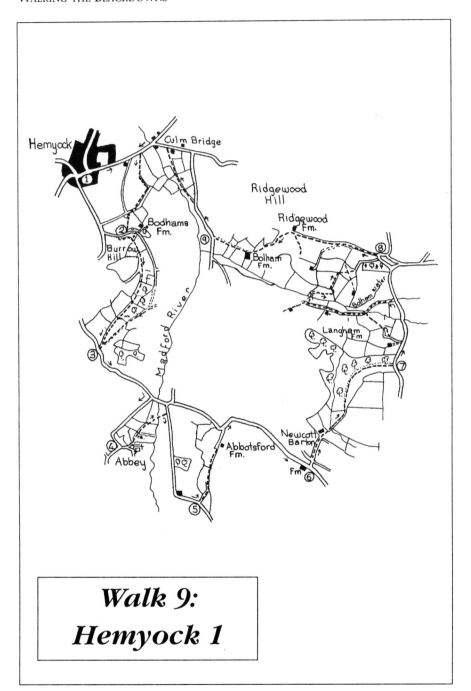

Walk 9: Hemyock 1

Walk 9: Hemyock 1

BURROW HILL • DUNKESWELL ABBEY • MADFORD •
MACKHAM • ABBOTSFORD FARM • NEWCOTT BARTON •
BOLHAM WATER • RIDGEWOOD HILL

Start: Village car park, Hemyock (next to Baptist Church)
Map ref: ST137132
Distance: 8 miles
Grading: Moderate, steep in places, can be muddy after wet weather
Refreshments: Provide your own. Alternatively, start walk at point
6 on map, then the Catherine Wheel Inn at Hemyock can be used
O.S. Maps: 1:50 000 Landranger- 193 (Taunton and Lyme Regis)
1:25 000 Pathfinder - ST1277 (01/11) Culm Valley

DIRECTIONS

(1) Turn right out of car park in an easterly direction and continue out
of village on road towards Culmbridge. Just past Culmbridge Farm,
turn right over stile on signed F.P. (Hemyock 33). Cross field to cattle
trough. Over a wire fence and turn left on farm track (a diversion) by
waymarks. Follow track for 120 yards to waymark post and turn right
over wire fence.

Proceed up left side of field to top. Bear right with top hedge to stile
and W.M. on left. Over and turn right on enclosed track to gate and
stile on left. Over and straight ahead on waymarked diversion on
muddy path, leading into a field. Cross field to gate and stile onto
road at F.P. sign.

(2) Turn right on road. Just before a farm, turn left over stile on signed
F.P. (Hemyock 38). Path climbs uphill between beech trees. Hemyock
is seen below with the Wellington Monument and Culmstock Beacon
across the valley. As the path levels out and enters a field, fork left
after a few yards between two banks. In 30 yards, pass through a gap
in bank on the left (W.M.), to enter another field.

Continue straight ahead on ridge, with hedge and bank on your right,
to gate. Through into second field and ahead to a stile. Proceed
through three more fields before arriving at a gate and F.P. sign and
onto a road in 40 yards.

(3) Turn left downhill on road. At bottom of hill, turn right at junction (signed to Dunkeswell Abbey, half a mile). Follow road to cross a ford.

(4) Turn left (signed to church and abbey) to water pump. Go through white gates and along signed F.P. (Dunkeswell 14), between clipped box hedges. Just before church, turn left across a small graveyard to stile in wall. Now follow a stream to a field bridge. Cross over and through a gate in 10 yards. Cross field to gate opposite. Through and bear right to cross F.B. over Madford River. Cross field to gate onto road and F.P. sign. Turn right on road. At Lower Mackham Farm, road bends sharp left uphill, past a cottage on the right.

(5) In 50 yards past cottage, turn left on enclosed track. As this bends left it is classified as a F.P. (Hemyock 43, part of). Follow this to end of track and enter field. Keep at the right edge to a gate (view through Madford River Valley and to Wellington Monument). Continue past Abbotsford Farm to road. Turn right for three quarters of a mile and turn left at a junction by a farm (Newcott Cross).

(6) In 50 yards, cross a cattle grid and follow drive to Newcott Barton Farm on F.P. (Clayhidon 46). Pass farmhouse and buildings to gate and join a short length of concrete farm road by wire fence. Turn left on track to gate. When this forks, take the left one and go over a stile by crossing gate. Continue through a pretty valley, to a gate. Then proceed through woody scrubland to gate, road and F.P. sign.

(7) Turn left downhill on road to entrance to Fields Farm. Turn left (90°) on farm track (not on entrance drive) on F.P. (Clayhidon 36). Continue to a gate across track. Then ahead to turn right into field in 30-40 feet. Now follow hedge to gate in 100 feet. Turn left through gate and bear half right across middle of field to gate and F.P. sign. Turn left on farm road (Clayhidon 34, part of) past Longham Farm. Follow this track for 400 yards to gate and F.P. sign on right. Turn right on F.P. (Clayhidon 33, part of) and down to a F.B. Cross and turn right by Bolham Water. Then follow to the left of a wet area to a gate. Through and turn left on F.P. (Clayhidon 30). Follow hedge to gate. Ahead, now, with hedge on your right. Turn right through next gate and go half left across middle of field to gate and F.P. sign. Proceed up

an enclosed track and join a road at a hairpin bend.

(8) Turn left in a few yards on drive to Battens Farm on F.P. (Clayhidon 29). Over a cattle grid and follow to a second cattle grid in a few hundred yards. Go straight ahead on signed F.P. to gate. Continue past the farm buildings and turn left through double gates on signed F.P. (Clayhidon 32). Follow a clear track down to gate. Through and keep at right side of a rough field to Bolham Farm. Through gate and past a 'collection' of machinery to join a farm road. Follow this to a road and F.P. sign.

(9) Turn right on road to a stile and F.P. sign on left (Hemyock 32 still). Over and walk through a field, parallel to Madford River to a stile at the far side of an old barn. Climb over and walk towards farm buildings. Go through the farmyard and out onto a road at F.P. sign. Turn left on road for half a mile back to Hemyock.

POINTS OF INTEREST

Hemyock: there is a monument and pump in the centre of the village which commemorates the reign of Victoria, the coronation of Edward VII and the restoration of peace in South Africa in 1902.

The castle was built by William the Conqueror and was given to the Hidon family (See Hidon Mill on walk 7).

The main industry in Hemyock has for some years been the processing of dairy goods at the St Ivel factory but this is to close.

The only remaining inn is the Catherine Wheel, named after the order of Knights of St Catherine, founded in 1063. This order was committed to protect pilgrims.

Hemyock's most recent claim to fame was when a couple from Cilla Black's 'Blind Date' programme were married in St Mary's church.

Dunkeswell Abbey: a Cistercian abbey. The manor of 'Donkewell' was granted to the Cistercian Order in 1201, by Lord William Brewer, for the foundation of an Abbey. Now only a ruined gatehouse and traces of walls remain.

The monks' fishponds now form part of a beautiful nature reserve with a restaurant adjacent called Fishponds.

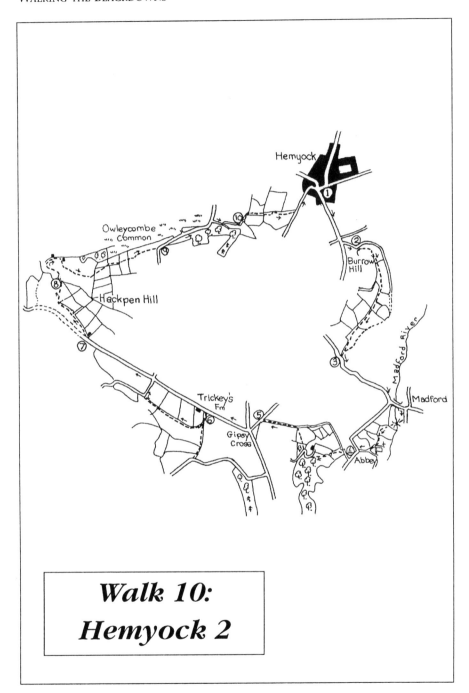

Walk 10:
Hemyock 2

Walk 10: Hemyock 2

BURROW HILL • MADFORD • DUNKESWELL ABBEY •
GIPSY CROSS • TRICKEY'S FARM • HACKPEN HILL •
OWLEYCOMBE COMMON

Start: Village car park, next to Baptist Church.
Map ref: ST137132
Distance: 7½ miles
Grading: Moderate
Refreshments: Provide your own, or start walk from near Gipsy Cross (near point 5 on map) and use the Inn at Hemyock
O.S. Maps: 1:50 000 Landranger - 193 (Taunton and Lyme Regis) 1:25 000 Pathfinder - ST01/11 (1277), Culm Valley

DIRECTIONS

(1) Turn left out of car park and then left again at the 'Victorian' pump and up High Street. Climb up out of Hemyock for just over 400 yards to a 'No through road' sign. Turn left on a lane and just past a farm, turn right over stile on signed F.P. (Hemyock 38).

(2) This path climbs steeply uphill between beech trees. Hemyock is seen below and Wellington Monument across the valley. As the path levels out and enters a field, fork left after a few yards, between two banks (W.M.). In 30-40 yards, pass through a gap in bank on the left, to another field, leading ahead on Burrow Hill, with a hedgebank on your right, to a gate. Through into second field to a stile. Pass through three more fields to a gate and F.P. sign. Reach road in 40 yards.

(3) Turn left and downhill. At the bottom, go past a right junction (signed to Dunkeswell) and across the Madford River bridge. Turn right at the next junction (signed to Mackham ¾ mile) and past some cottages and a barn to the first gate on the right and a signed F.P. (Hemyock 46). Then cross a field to a F.B. over the Madford River. The F.P. then continues as (Dunkeswell 14). Bear left across field to a gate (W.M.). Go through the middle of the next field to a gate. Go through and in a few yards, cross a stream, (W.M.) and follow it to

enter the church graveyard, over a stile in wall. Cross to a gap and turn right between box hedges to the white entrance gates of the church and Dunkeswell Abbey at a F.P. sign. Go past a water pump, a left junction and a telephone box, to Abbey Cross.

(4) Turn left and follow the road to a white house. Turn right on an enclosed track called Burnsome Lane to first gate on left and a F.P. sign (Dunkeswell 18). N.B. This is a diverted route. Turn through gate and bear right across corner of field to gate. Through and bear left to F.B. and stile. Cross a small area of woodland to enter field. Turn right uphill across field to meet a hedgeline to the left of buildings. Leave through a gate and turn left up a farm track to a crossing farm road. Cross straight over to enter woods on a waymarked F.P. Bear right up and across this small wood to a stile. Enter a field and bear left across a slope to top corner. Climb over stile and ahead up an enclosed track (continuation of Burnsome Lane) to a gateway onto road at a F.P. sign.

(5) Turn left for 200 yards to Gipsy Cross. Continue over the crossroad for 400 yards to Trickeys Farm.

(6) Turn left on an enclosed track on signed F.P. (Uffculme 36) and follow this to enter a field. Bear right and follow waymarked F.P. along Hackpen Hill (fine views across to Blackborough, where the landmark of the church has been demolished) to a gate. Cross a third field to a stile and F.P. sign at a road bend. Turn right to Leigh Cross. Turn left and proceed for half a mile to Hayden Farm and Hayden End.

(7) Fork right on signed F.P. (Uffculme 29), and follow a clear track through woods to an enclosed track on your right, by a gate. Go past this and continue on F.P. for 300 yards to where path begins to dip downhill. Here fork right over a bank (W.M.'d) and along a wire fence to second beech tree. Turn right over a stile (W.M.), and straight across field to a gate (W.M.).

(8) Through and ahead on F.P. (Culmstock 3a) for 40 yards. Turn left on a track going downhill through bracken, and then woods. Towards end of woods, join and walk on a bank (to avoid a wet area). Just short of wood bottom, turn right and follow waymarks along an enclosed track (very wet). Continue past a cottage to a farm. Turn right by farmhouse and follow a clear path up through Owleycombe Common.

At the top, follow waymarks across the common in an easterly direction to a gate (W.M.). Enter a field at parish boundary on F.P. (Hemyock 23) and follow left edge to stile (W.M.). Over and ahead through bracken on waymarked F.P. At a crossing hedgeline go over a stile on right to enter a field. Keep to the left edge to a stile. Over and follow a clear path at edge of woods. Go through a gap at end of woods into a field and continue to far end. Go over a stile onto a road and F.P. sign (fine views of Culm valley).

(9) Turn left on road and downhill for nearly half a mile. Turn right on an enclosed track. Fork left and follow to a road.

(10) Turn left on signed F.P. (Hemyock 24). At the end of this track, go through a gate and across a field to another gate. Pass through and turn right to follow hedge down to a stile. Then go down the left side of a third field to a stile and F.P. sign onto a road, near a bungalow. Turn left on road and follow to Hemyock. Go past the Catherine Wheel Inn and ahead back to car park.

POINTS OF INTEREST

Hemyock village and Dunkeswell Abbey: see walk 9 for details.

Dunkeswell Abbey

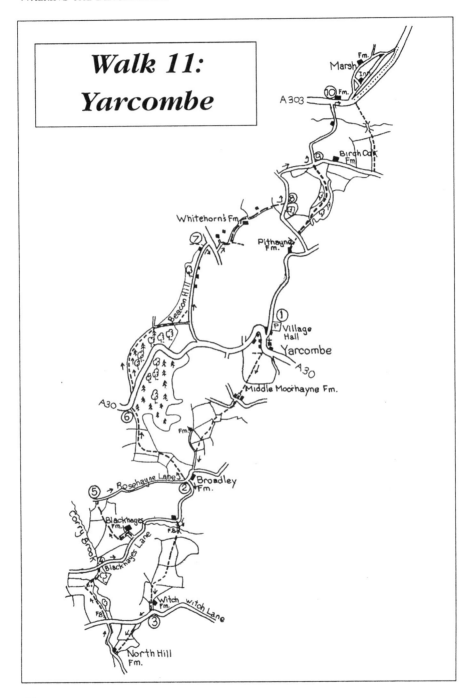

Walk 11:
Yarcombe

Walk 11: Yarcombe

BROADLEY FARM • NORTH HILL FARM • BLACKHAYES LANE •
ROSEHAYES LANE • BEACON HILL • MARSH • BIRCH HILL

Start: Village Hall, Yarcombe
Map ref: ST246083
Distance: 8 miles
Grading: Moderate
Refreshments: The Flintlock Inn, Marsh and Yarcombe Inn
O.S. Maps: 1:50 000 Landranger - 193 (Taunton)
1:25 000 Pathfinder - ST20/30 (1297) and ST21/31 (1278)

DIRECTIONS

(1) Turn left from car park and go past the church to the Yarcombe
Inn. Turn left on the A30 and follow downhill. Turn right opposite
the vicarage on signed F.P. (Yarcombe No. 20) up an enclosed track for
20 yards to a stile. Follow along the left side of field to stile. Cross the
next field to gate and stile opposite. Keep near left side of a third field
to a gate and track leading to a road and F.P. sign. Cross straight over,
and along a private road. In 40 yards, when farm drive turns right, go
ahead (W.M.) through gate into field. Turn half right and cross field to
stile and waymark near bend in hedgeline. Over stile and walk half
left across corner of field by a dell to join the hedgeline at a bend.
Follow this hedge for 30 yards to a gate. Through and cross the middle
of next field to gate in hedge opposite (W.M.). Through onto
(Yarcombe 19, part of) and climb up through a small field to a stile.
Over and turn left on a farm track to a road at a bend and F.P. sign. Go
straight ahead on road for 100 yards.

(2) Turn left by Broadley Farm. Follow this lane to a second right
bend, near some farm buildings. Turn left on signed F.P. (Yarcombe
No. 7). Go straight across a small field to a F.B. in right hedgeline.
Cross over F.B. and ahead across field to a gate and proceed uphill
through the middle of field. Pass to the left of a small dell and join the
left hedge at a gate. Through and turn right. Follow hedge to a gate to
the left of a barn. Continue uphill to gate. Pass through this and turn

left through another gate and cross field on F.P. (Stockland 3) to Witch Farm. Then over a stile and out on drive to road and F.P. sign.

(3) Turn right and continue downhill. Look out for a stile and F.P. (Stockland No. 10, part of) on left. Cross stile and proceed down left side of field to gate. Through and follow hedge down towards North Hill Farm to stile and F.P. sign. Turn right on road. Follow this to a junction and bridge. Pass through a gate opposite on signed F.P. (Stockland No. 5) to a F.B. in 30-40 yards. Cross over Corry Brook and turn right to follow the brook to a gate leading into a wooded area. Follow the brook for a further 30 yards, bearing slightly left to cross a tributary of Corry Brook. Turn right on a diverted F.P. (Upottery No. 14). Follow the brook in a wooded area to a small gate. Through and follow to a field bridge. Cross and continue to a gate. Turn right on road.

(4) Continue uphill and around a left bend. Turn left on signed B.W. (Yarcombe No. 11) to Blackhayes Farm. Follow between duck ponds to gate. Then straight across the field and uphill to a gate. Pass ahead in another field to a gate leading onto a road.

(5) Turn right (Rosehayne Lane) to pass a farm. Continue to a road junction at Broadley Farm at point 2 (previously passed)

(2) Turn left through gate on F.P. (Yarcombe No. 18) and follow this stony track up and across a field to a gate. Keep with this track for 150 yards to second gate and proceed on same track which soon bends to the right and up across field to enter woods. Walk through the woods until the A30 is reached.

(6) Cross straight over (taking care at dangerous bend) on signed F.P. (Yarcombe No. 26) and follow a clear track over Beacon Hill in woods for half a mile. At a junction, fork right downhill. Turn left into a field in 100 yards before a road (at end of woods). Go through this field to a road and F.P. sign. Turn left and follow past three cottages to a T junction.

(7) Turn right and in 50 yards turn left down a signed B.W. (Yarcombe No. 31). In a further 50 yards, turn right down concreted farm road (still on Yarcombe 31) to Whitehorn Farm. Continue on hedged B.W. for 50 yards to gate. Enter a field and go past a small barn and on to a

gate by a wall. Cross the next field to a gate, road and F.P. sign.

(8) Turn left on road and then right at next junction.

(9) Turn left at next junction and follow downhill to cottages and then up to main road (A303) at Marsh. Turn right, without crossing road to stile and signed F.P. (Yarcombe No. 42) (N.B. For refreshments, cross A303 into Marsh for Flintlock Inn or Cottage Inn).

(10) Turn right of A303 over stile and down, slightly left, across field to field bridge. Bear left up next field to gate. Through and follow up right side of field to gate, road and F.P. sign. Turn right on road to next junction (previously passed).

(9) Opposite junction, turn left on signed F.P. (Yarcombe No. 45) and cross field, slightly left uphill to corner of a small wood on Birch Hill. Follow along beside wood. Towards the end of this small strip of woodland, bear left, down to gate in corner of field. Through and along edge of next field to a stile and steps onto road and F.P. sign. Cross straight over to a stile opposite. Cross next field to join a hedgeline. Follow this down to a stile and steps in corner, at Pithayne Farm. Turn right on road and continue back to village hall car park at Yarcombe. (N.B. Go past church for refreshments at the Yarcombe Inn).

POINTS OF INTEREST

Yarcombe village is dominated by the tall, 14th century church tower and lays astride one of the two main routes from Somerset to Honiton, the A30. There are unrivalled views down the chequered patterned fields of the Yarty valley. The Yarcombe estate was acquired by Sir Francis Drake in the reign of Elizabeth I and remains the property of descendants of Sir Francis.

Yarcombe Inn: 14th century inn that used to be a guest house for the monks of Otterton Priory. It was later called the Angel Inn. It then became the Yarcombe Inn when used by stage-coach passengers to and from Exeter.

Many local names on the map indicate former industries e.g. Old Forge, Mill Green, Foundry Farm.

Unusual sporting activities occur in the village, including barrel rolling, steel ball throwing, terrier racing and pig racing. The East Devon Sheepdog Trials are held here in July.

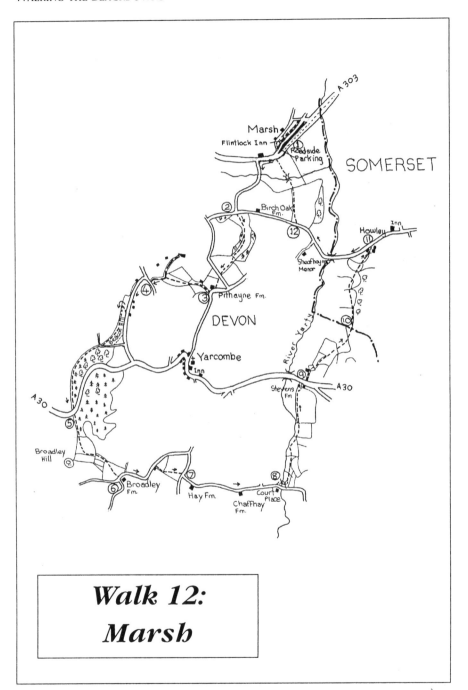

Walk 12: Marsh

Walk 12: Marsh

Birch Hill • Pithayne Farm • Beacon Hill • Broadley Farm • River Yarty • Howley • Sheafhayne Cross • Marsh

Start: Road parking, top end of Marsh village
Map ref: ST254104
Distance: 7 ½ miles
Grading: Easy to moderate.
Refreshments: Inn at Howley or Flintlock Inn at Marsh
O.S. Maps: 1:50 000 Landranger - 193 (Taunton and Lyme Regis)
1:25 000 Pathfinder - ST 21/31 (1278) Ilminster;
ST 20/30 (1297) Chard

DIRECTIONS

(1) Walk up to junction with A303 (No exit for traffic sign). Cross this busy main road, above dual carriageway, with care, and turn right to a road junction. Turn left and follow down a steep hill to a thatched cottage. Then climb steeply up to a T junction in 400 yards.

(2) Cross straight over on signed F.P. (Yarcombe 45). Climb across field to join a hedgerow and bear left with this, to follow along side of woods. Towards the end of field, bear left down to corner of field by lower gate. Through and follow left edge of field to stile, steps and F.P. sign. Descend, and cross over road to signed F.P. (still Yarcombe 45). Cross over stile and ahead to join a hedgerow. Follow this down to a stile in corner, at Pithayne Farm. Cross stile and down steps to road and F.P. sign.

(3) Turn right on road and in 20-30 yards, turn right on F.P. (Yarcombe 33). Follow enclosed track, past a farm cottage on right to a gate ahead. Then keep at left side of a small field to a gate. Through and bear right and up across field to metal gate (W.M.) at top, leading onto a concrete farm road. Turn left on this and continue to a T junction. Turn left to reach a road and B.W. sign in 50 yards.

(4) Turn right on road for 50 yards. Then turn left at junction. Follow road for 300 yards to just before second cottage on left. Here, turn

back right up a very steep path. On reaching the top, ahead to turn left on a clear track, just before a gate. Follow this track through woods on Beacon Hill for 600 yards to a crossing track. Go straight over on F.P. (Yarcombe 26) and follow track for ½ mile in woods to main road (A30) and F.P. sign.

(5) Cross straight over at blind bend, taking care and ahead on signed F.P. (Yarcombe 18), through woods on clear track to gate in 250 yards (W.M.). A superb view now greets you of the Yarty valley as you descend on clear track through three fields to a road junction at Broadleys Farm.

(6) Turn left on road and then right at bend. Continue downhill to farm and bend left. In 100 yards, turn right over stile onto signed F.P. (Yarcombe 24) by a cottage with a green roof. Cross field to a small gate and stile. Bear left across next field to gate, stile and F.P. sign at a road.

(7) Cross straight over road to junction opposite, by a bungalow. Continue down road passing Hay and Chaffhay Farm. Then cross a ford and follow road uphill to a left junction. Go past this and downhill past Court Place to a F.B.

(8) Cross over the River Yarty onto F.P. (Membury 14) and across a field to a F.P. sign by a gate. Turn left in field and ahead to a stile near corner. Cross second field to a gate. Go through and over a ditch. Cross a third field by River Yarty. Towards the end of field, bear right to a gate. Go through and turn left by a river and cross fourth field to a stile. Cross fifth field to Stevens Farm. Go through a small gate and out onto the A30 and F.P. sign.

(9) Turn right on road and in 50 yards, turn left on signed F.P. (Membury 15). Follow along an enclosed track to gate at Bridge Meadows Farm. Go through two muddy and mucky yards to gate ahead into field (not through gate on left). Turn right and follow hedge to corner of field in 50 yards. Climb over stile into next field and turn left to follow hedge. When this bends left by a dell continue straight across field to gate and stile. Over and bear left across field to stile on county border with Somerset.

(10) Over and keep to right side of next field on F.P. (Whitestaunton

CH29/7). (Beacon Hill, walked earlier, is away across the valley). Cross a removed hedgerow (a few trees remaining) and bear left across field to gate. Cross next field to gate and ahead on track to gate. Through and follow past farm buildings to gate. Go through farmyard of Howley Farm to road (N.B. If pub at Howley is needed for refreshments, then turn right).

(11) Turn left down lane and across a road bridge over the River Yarty. Proceed uphill past a left junction (Sheafhayne Cross) and uphill to a signed F.P.

(12) Turn right on this F.P. (Yarcombe 42). Cross a large field at left side to gate ahead in corner (not gate on left). Through and bear left across and down field to gate and field bridge. Over and up across field to stile and F.P. sign on A303. Cross road and back into Marsh.

POINTS OF INTEREST

Yarcombe: see walk 11.

Sheafhayne Manor used to house heirlooms of Sir Francis Drake

Yarcombe

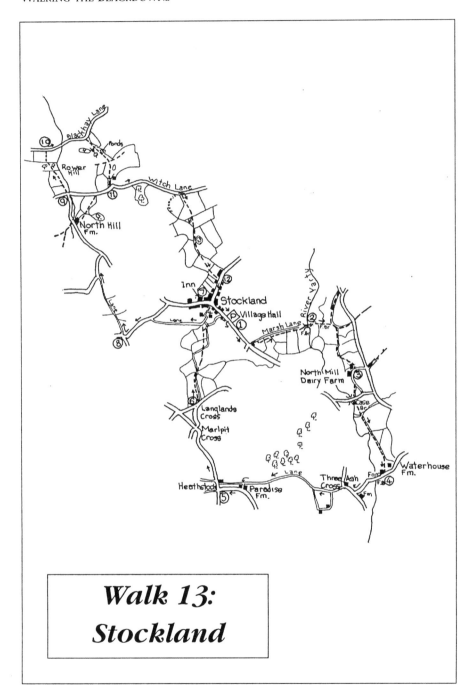

Walk 13:
Stockland

Walk 13: Stockland

(FIGURE OF EIGHT WALK)

PART 1 (4 MILES): MARSH LANE • NORTH MILL DAIRY FARM • CASE BRIDGE • WATERHOUSE FARM • THREE ASH CROSS • HEATHSTOCK • MARLPIT CROSS • STOCKLAND
PART 2 (4 MILES): HORNSHAYES KNAP CROSS • NORTH HILL FARM • BLACKHAYES LANE • ROWER HILL • WITCH FARM • WITCH LANE • STOCKLAND

Start: (Part 1) Stockland village hall car park
Map ref: ST246046
Distance: Total of 8 miles (4 miles each part)
Grading: Easy, but one steep climb from Three Ash Cross.
Refreshments: The Inn at Stockland
O.S. Maps: 1:50 000 Landranger - 193 (Taunton and Lyme Regis)
1:25 000 Pathfinder - ST20/30 (1297) Chard

DIRECTIONS: PART 1 – 4 MILES

(1) Turn left out of car park. Just past a right turning in 400 yards turn left on an enclosed track on signed F.P. (Stockland 6). In 50 feet turn right over stile and then left to follow at the left edge of five fields to a F.B. over the River Yarty, at the parish boundary.

(2) F.P. now continues (as Membury 12). Cross a small field to another F.B. Then bear right to a fence in hedge. Over and cross a small field to pass over a ditch. Then follow the hedge on your right to a double fence and ditch. Turn right over fence on F.P. (Membury 10, part of), and follow at the left edge of a large field to the third gate on the left. Through and bear right across field to buildings. Climb over a stile in wire fence. Cross an area of stored machinery and out onto a road and F.P. sign.

(3) Turn right and past North Mill Dairy Farm to a signed F.P. (still Membury 10). Turn right on this, through gate and follow with a ditch on your left. Bear left across a small field to a F.B. and ahead to a stile onto road at Case Bridge. Cross straight over road and over a stile and F.B. to continue on Membury 10. Cross three fields to Waterhouse Farm. Pass through grounds of this farmhouse conversion to a road.

(4) Turn right down an old lane to a ford, over the River Yarty. If too deep to cross, then turn left over a fence just before the ford and ahead over two F.B.s to rejoin the lane. Forward, to cross another ford and then proceed to a T junction. Turn right and uphill past Three Ashes Farm (home of Suffolk horses). Fork left at junction (Three Ash Cross) up a 'No through road'. At a left bend continue straight ahead up an 'old road' and climb steeply uphill. Turn right at a T junction (N.B. avoid a left turn in a few yards) and continue up an enclosed track for nearly half a mile. Near the end of this, bear left up to Paradise Farm and a road. Turn right and on downhill to a crossroads at Heathstock.

(5) Turn right past Heathstock Farm and a left junction. Continue to Marlpit crossroads at letter box, and turn right. Just past a back junction on your left, turn left over a stile on a signed F.P. (Stockland 25).

(6) Follow down enclosed track to gate. Pass through this and another field gate and ahead down field in direction of Stockland church. At F.P. sign go through a gate on left, 50 yards before bottom corner into next field. Bear right through field. Cross a ditch and ahead to gate and F.P. sign. Through and in 50 feet turn right and follow road to a T junction. Turn right to village hall car park.

N.B. If refreshments are now required, leave car park and turn right on road and over a crossroads to the pub in Stockland at point (7) on map.

DIRECTIONS: PART 2 – 4 MILES

(1) From village hall car park, turn right to crossroads in Stockland. Turn left down to church (N.B. turn right after coming to this spot from pub). Go through the churchyard to gate into lane and past cottages and Churchstyle Farm. Just past the farm continue ahead on track to gate in 20 yards. Do not go through gate, but turn right up enclosed track for 500 yards to a road. Turn left for 400 yards to a left junction.

(8) Opposite this junction, turn right up an enclosed track. Follow this for 600 yards to a road. Turn right and continue to a T junction (North Hill Lane). Turn left for 400 yards to North Hill Farm. Go past

the farm for a further 400 yards to a T junction at a bridge.

(9) Go straight over the junction to gate and signed F.P. (Stockland 5). Proceed to a F.B. in 30-40 yards. Cross over Corry Brook and follow it to a gate leading into a wooded area. Follow the stream for 30 yards, bearing slightly left to cross a tributary of Corry Brook. Turn right on a diverted F.P. (Upottery No. 14). Follow brook in a wooded area to a small gate. Through and follow to a field bridge. Cross and continue to gate.

(10) Turn right on road. In 300 yards at left bend, turn right through gate on signed F.P. (Yarcombe 6). Follow up left side of field to gate. Go through and ahead on track past two ponds to gate. Through and cross field on F.P. (Stockland 3) to stile at Witch Farm. Follow farm drive over a cattle grid to road and F.P. sign.

(11) Turn left on road (Witch Lane) for half a mile to a left bend. Turn right on signed F.P. (Stockland 19). Over steps and stile. Follow down hedge. When this bends to right continue ahead across field to gate. Pass through and down the right edge of field to a small gate. Continue down the right side of the next field to gate ahead. Through and bear left across field to gate, in direction of houses. Go through and across field to the right of houses to gate, road and F.P. sign.

(12) Turn right through village to crossroads and turn left back to village hall car park.

POINTS OF INTEREST

Stockland is situated in the Yarty Valley and is a parish of scattered farms, bounded on the east by the River Yarty and on the west by the Umborne Brook. The village became part of Devon in 1842. Prior to this it was in the county of Dorset, an island surrounded by Devon. There are two Iron Age camps in the area and an abundance of tools and axes have been found.

The church is quite large and was built in the 14th and 15th centuries. There are an unusually large number of houses which date back to the 15th and 16th centuries.

At one time smuggling was rife in the area, even though the village is twelve miles from the sea.

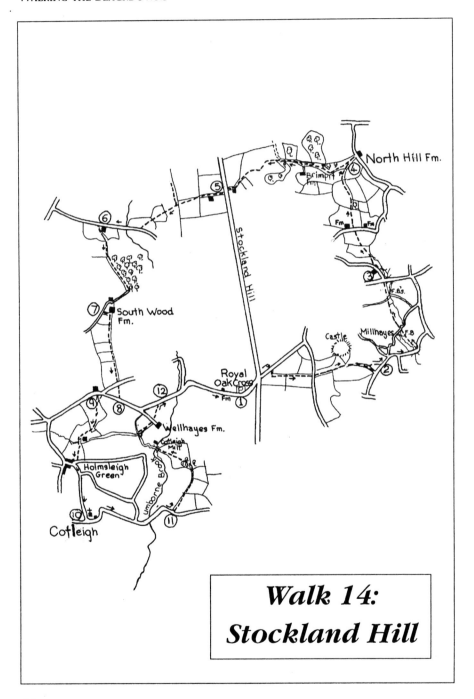

Walk 14:
Stockland Hill

Walk 14: Stockland Hill

(ROYAL OAK CROSS)

MILLHAYES • NORTH HILL FARM • BUCEHAYES COMMON •
SOUTHWOOD FARM • COTLEIGH BRIDGE

Start: Road verge, 200 yards down Cotleigh side of Royal Oak Cross
Map ref. ST221033
Distance: 7½ miles
Refreshments: Provide your own
Grading: Moderate
O.S. Maps: 1:50,000 Landranger - 193 (Taunton and Lyme Regis)
1:25,000 Pathfinder - ST20/30 (1297)

DIRECTIONS

(1) Proceed uphill for 200 yards to Royal Oak Cross. Cross straight
over in Stockland direction for 100 yards. Turn right on signed F.P.
(Stockland 22) and across to stile. Over and turn left down the side of
two fields to road and F.P. sign. Cross straight over to gate. Through
and down the right side of field. When the hedgerow ends, cross
remainder of field to a gate. Follow down an enclosed track (fine view
of Horner Hill). When this bends right, turn left through gate and
bear half right, down and across corner of field to gate onto road and
F.P. sign near telephone box.

(2) Turn left on road and bear right past a junction. Continue
downhill, past a right junction. Cross a ford and turn left to gate on
signed F.P. (Stockland 11). Follow through field by Corry Brook to F.B.
Then follow brook to a lane. Turn left uphill and in a few yards turn
right on signed F.P. (Still Stockland 11). Go through garden of cottage.
Path follows by a millstream to a stile. Now follow across a small
paddock between the millstream and Corry Brook to stile. Continue
through a second paddock to gate, road and F.P. sign. Turn right for a
few yards, then left on signed F.P. by a stream to F.B. Cross F.B. and
turn right in field. Keep at right edge to reach a stile by a house.
Ahead to road and F.P. sign.

(3) Turn right, and in a few yards, left at a junction. Just past a
farmhouse on left, turn right on signed F.P. (Stockland 10). Turn half

left across field to a stile. Over this and across a ditch into field. Keep near to right side to gate 40 feet from corner. Cross the middle of next field to gate, road and F.P. sign. Cross road and ahead through farmyard into field. Cross the field to stile and F.B. Over and along right side of two fields to gateway.

(4) Through gateway and turn left on F.P. (Stockland 16). When fence bends right, go straight ahead to gate in 50 yards. Cross field to gate opposite. Follow farm road for 150 yards. Then fork left on track (still Stockland 16) to enter woods through gate. On leaving the woods, bear left on clear track in field to top of hill to a gate by a bungalow. Cross the next field to gate, road and F.P. sign.

(5) Turn left on Stockland Hill road and in a few yards turn right on drive to Park Farm (Stockland 15). Go past the farmhouse and out on a concreted farm track to a gate. Ahead on track and enter a field by squeezing between two posts supporting an electric fence. Descend to stile in hedge. Cross this and a crossing track, to continue on a signed F.P. between bracken, gorse and scrubland to a cottage. Pass ahead in front of the cottage, and down a track to a gate. Enter field and cross to a gate opposite (W.M.). Descend half left across next field to a stile and F.P. sign by a bungalow. Turn right on road and pass two cottages before crossing a ford. Now climb uphill to gate and F.P. sign on left, just past Wakeley's Cottage.

(6) Turn left through gates on this signed F.P. (Cotleigh 18) and keep at left side of field to a stile (W.M.) Over and ahead on a wooded F.P. Best to walk on a bank as F.P. can be very wet at times. Continue to, and cross above, a deep ditch, and in a few yards more, climb over a fence. Now follow a clear F.P. near right edge of woods. When this ends, turn right on track. Pass a cottage to your right.

(7) Turn left on F.P. (Cotleigh 14a) signed to Southwood Farm. When the track bears left to house and buildings, turn right to pond. Circumnavigate to right of this and over a fence. Now cross four fields in a southerly direction before reaching a road and F.P. sign. Cross straight over road and ahead over a fence on signed F.P. (Cotleigh 14). Cross one field on this F.P. to a road and F.P. sign.

(8) N.B. If a shorter walk of 6 miles only is required, turn left and

follow road for one mile back to start.

To continue the full walk of 7½ miles, turn right on road. Go past a junction on right.

(9) Go through a gate on your left, opposite a pair of cottages on a diverted F.P. (Cotleigh 11). Bear right on a track to a gate in 50 feet. Through and turn left. (You are now on correct route). Proceed through middle of field on contour line (i.e. towards a barn on horizon). Near far side of field, bear right to gate. Go through and bear left across field to a gate to the right of a thatched cottage. Through and up across field to gate, road and F.P sign. Turn right to Holmsleigh Green. Turn left at junction and after a bend, turn right on an enclosed track. Follow this down and over a ford. Then up to a road at Cotleigh church.

(10) Turn left and on down a narrow and twisting lane. Pass a left junction and on to cross a bridge over Umborne Brook. Climb up and round a right bend to a gate and F.P. sign on left.

(11) Turn left on this signed F.P. (Stockland 8), and across two fields to gate in corner. Through and ahead to stile on left (W.M.). Over and across small wooded area to another stile (W.M.). Over and walk down the left side of field. Bear right at a waymarked post, across to a stile and waymark. Climb over and turn down left to a stile (W.M.). Ahead for a few yards through gorse and brambles to cross the Umborne Brook by a F.B. The brook is the parish boundary and so continues as F.P. (Cotleigh 19), past cottages to gate and F.P. sign. Climb uphill on a lane. At a left bend, turn right on an enclosed track. Follow down to a bridge over a stream. Turn right through gate (W.M.) on farm track (Cotleigh 13). In 50 yards climb over fence on left. Then continue at right edge of field to gate near Wellhayes Farm. Cross farm road and through the left hand of two gates (waymarked). Go across middle of field to gate, road and F.P. sign.

(12) Turn right and follow road down and up for nearly a mile, back to start below Royal Oak Cross.

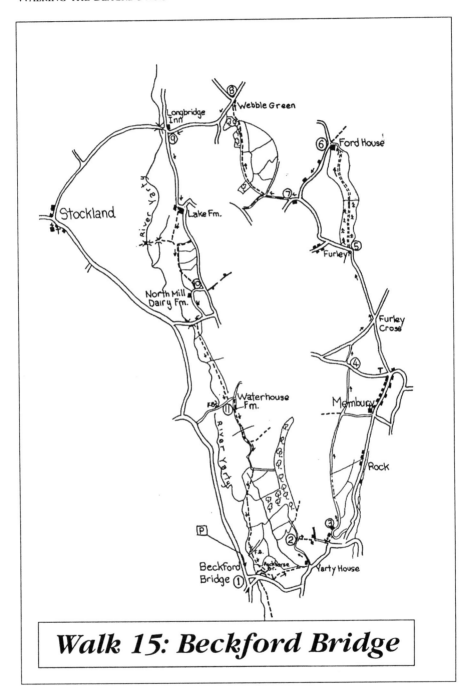

Walk 15: Beckford Bridge

Walk 15: Beckford Bridge

CLEAVE HILL • GOYLE ACRE LANE • FURLEY CROSS • FORDE HOUSE • THORNE FARM • LONGBRIDGE INN • NORTH MILL FARM • RIVER YARTY

Start: Roadside parking on Stockland to Axminster road, near Beckford Bridge

Map ref: ST264014

Distance: 8 miles

Grading: Moderate, muddy in places

Refreshments: The Longbridge Inn

O.S. Maps: 1:50 000 Landranger - 193 (Taunton and Lyme Regis) 1:25 000 Pathfinder - 1297 (Chard), ST 20/30

DIRECTIONS

(1) From road side parking (facing Axminster direction) turn left to River Yarty. Just short of road bridge, turn left for a few yards and then cross River Yarty over Beckford packhorse bridge. Rejoin the road that crosses the river. Turn left through second gate on signed F.P. (Membury 11). Cross field in direction of sign to far narrow corner. Cross a ditch and stile onto a road (F.P. sign). Turn left and in a few yards (just before Yarty House) turn right on enclosed path. Continue for 500 yards to a gate.

(2) Turn right through gate on F.P. (Membury 42). Go straight across a field to a thatched white cottage. Pass through gate and follow a private road to a gate. Between this and a road, turn left on signed F.P. (still Membury 42), and climb steeply through bracken and woods to a bungalow. Come out onto the drive to a thatched hotel and cottage.

(3) Turn left on the drive and go past both of these and fork left on an enclosed track to gate. This now continues as an open track through three fields to a gate, then becomes enclosed again (N.B. Just inside the second field is a metal gate leading into a Quaker burial ground). Follow the enclosed track past a turning on the right (leading to Membury church in 300 yards).

(4) On reaching a road, turn left for 100 yards and then right on an enclosed track. Turn right at next junction with a road, and follow to

Furley Cross. Turn left for just under ½ mile. Continue downhill avoiding the first enclosed track on right.

(5) Turn right up second enclosed track (50 yards before, and in sight of, a bridge). Follow track, which opens out and leads through a plantation and into a field. Keep on this clear track. Join a surfaced track coming in from the right and continue to a gate. Proceed down, past some cottages to a road at Forde House.

(6) Turn left and on past Rose Cottage. At a road junction, turn right past Thorne Farm.

(7) At the end of farm buildings, fork right on enclosed B.W. (Membury 29). This track rises uphill, and just before it descends round to the left, fork right for a few yards to the right of two gates on F.P. (Membury 25, part of). Keep at the left side of a long field (with fine views to Beacon Hill) to a small gate. Go through a second field, and through a gate at the far end. Bear left downhill and at the end of woods on left, in 50 yards, bear right on clear path to gate, road and F.P. sign.

(8) Turn left on road and then right at a junction (signed to Stockland and Yarcombe, fine views to Beacon Hill and Yarcombe). Follow this road downhill to the Longbridge Inn.

(9) Turn left (signed to Membury). Follow the road past a F.P. on your left. Just before a T junction turn right through the farmyard of Lake Farm on signed F.P. (Membury 10). N.B. Go through the double gates (not in front of farmhouse). Proceed through a second gate into field and keep at left side. In 50 yards, go through gate and cross field to a double fence in hedge. Over and across a long field to the third gate on the left. Through, and bear right towards buildings. Go over a stile in wire fence, to the left of a tin barn. Follow the wire fence for a few yards. Then out through a yard to a road and F.P. sign.

(10) Turn right and past North Mill Dairy Farm. Turn right on signed F.P. (still Membury 10). Keep to the left side of field to a stile and F.B. in far corner. In a few more yards cross over a stile onto a road. Cross over a stile and F.B. opposite. Walk across a field, with the River Yarty on your right to a stream, and gate, 40 yards from the river. Go across a second field to a gate. Then cross a third field to Waterhouse Farm

(now a private residence). Pass through on possible diversion to a road and turn right.

(11) In a few yards turn left to follow an enclosed track on signed F.P. (still Membury 10) for 50 yards to gate. This track now crosses a field as an open track to gate. Continue with track now enclosed again. On leaving this track, go straight ahead down a concrete farm road. Follow through Yarty Farm and ahead on enclosed track. In 100 yards track bends left but continue straight ahead through a gate into a field. Cross this field, bearing right, to a gate about 30-40 yards from far end of field. Cross the next field, bearing half left to the far right corner of this long field to a stile and F.B. Over and follow the River Yarty to road and F.P. sign. Turn right and return to your parking spot, near Beckford Bridge.

POINTS OF INTEREST

Beckford Bridge: an old packhorse bridge over the River Yarty.

Membury village lies below the ancient hill fort, Membury Castle, whose ditches and ramparts remain to this day. It is essentially a farming village, with many sheep about.

There is still a village school, next to the church, but the number of children is falling, which is causing concern to the population. There are small local industries and businesses, such as a trout farm, toy and candlemaker and basket weaver while cider is made by several people. The village thatcher has now retired. There is still a village shop.

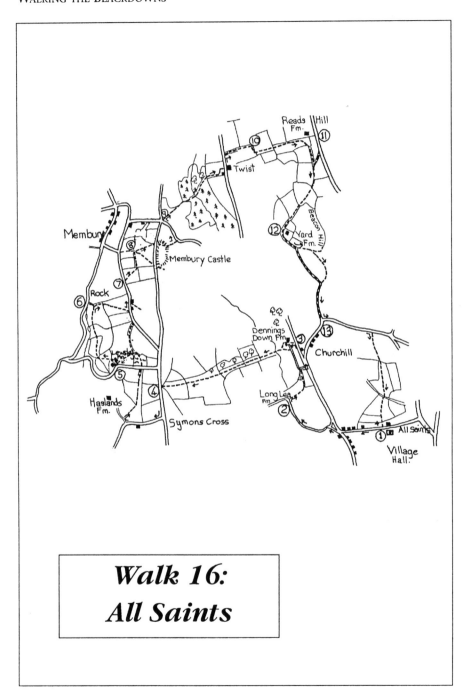

Walk 16: All Saints

Walk 16: All Saints

SMALLRIDGE • LONG LEA FARM • DENNINGS DOWN FARM •
SYMONS CROSS • ROCK • GREEN DOWN • MEMBURY CASTLE •
TWIST • READS HILL FARM • YARD FARM

Start: Village hall car park
Map ref: ST305011
Distance: 9 miles
Grading: Moderate, but with a few steep but short climbs
Refreshments: Provide your own. Alternatively start from
Membury village and use pub in Smallridge
O.S. Maps: 1:50 000 Landranger - 193 (Taunton and Lyme Regis)
1:25 000 Pathfinder - ST20/30 (1297) Chard

DIRECTIONS

(1) Turn left out of car park and continue through village to a T junction. Turn right and in 50 yards turn left. Then bear right up a 'No through road'. Keep on this lane for nearly half a mile to Long Lea Farm.

(2) Just before farm, turn right over stile into field on signed F.P. (Chardstock 69). Climb up field to join a hedgerow. Continue up the remaining 100 yards of field to gate (W.M.). Through and bear left to join a track to gate (W.M.). Follow the track uphill to join a lane at a bend and F.P. sign. Turn right for 100 yards to T junction and turn left. Go past a right turning to a signed F.P. on the left.

(3) Turn left through small gate on signed F.P. (Membury 6) and down a steep field to gate. Through and turn right past a cottage (W.M.) on track and down a concreted farm road. Turn left at gates (W.M.) and bear left down to stream. Cross over (W.M.) and through gate. Ahead across two fields at the left side followed by four fields at the right edge. Turn right on the drive of Park Farm, near duck pond. Cross cattle grid to road and F.P. sign.

(4) Turn left on road to Symons Cross. Turn right at this junction for quarter of a mile to entrance drive of Hasland Farm (F.P. and B.W. signs). Turn right along drive on F.P. (Membury 8) for 50 yards. Turn right over stile and cross field bearing left. Avoid a stile on right in

wire fence (not a public F.P.), but continue to corner of field in 50 yards. Through gate and follow hedge around top side of field (fine views to Yarty valley), bearing left with it to stile and small gate on right. Cross over and turn right up a steep bank for a few yards and turn left by poultry sheds. Follow this surfaced track past the sheds. At the end of the buildings, head towards farm bungalow. Follow the garden fence and then fork down steep bank, through brambles and ahead for 30-40 yards to stile and F.P. sign. Cross road to stile and F.P. sign opposite. Over and bear left through a very rough field of grass, reeds and brambles. Pass a pond and continue to top left corner to fence. Climb over and follow hedge for about 100 yards.

(5) Then turn down back hard left across field to Lewsley Farm below on unsigned F.P. (Membury 20). Cross over F.B. (plank) and stile onto drive and F.P. sign. Immediately turn right on F.P. (Membury 17), up through Lewsley Farm and two gates. Cross a field, bearing slightly right to a stile opposite (W.M.). Continue down through a valley on clear F.P. to cross a hedgerow through a gap. Cross field to gate. Through and across another field (with trout farm on left) to a small gate in lower right corner.

(6) Through gate onto F.P. (Membury 18). Climb up through field, keeping at the left side to a gate, stile and W.M. Over and turn left on farm track for a few yards, and just past a garage, turn right through gate (W.M.). Bear right, up and across a large field with hedges removed to a stile and F.P. signed at top. Turn left on road and past a cottage and bungalow with a F.P. sign between them. Ignore this and continue along road for 300 yards to the next F.P. sign on right.

(7) Turn right over stile on signed F.P. (Membury 24) into field and bear left across field to top corner, passing an old quarry, to stile and W.M. Over stile and turn left near edge of field to a stile in wire fence, 50 feet from hedge.

(8) Do not go over this stile or the one in left hedge but turn right to a gate near farmhouse and out onto a road and F.P. sign. Turn left on road. Then opposite a drive on left turn right over a stile and F.P. sign. Continue up a steep field to Membury Castle. Go through a gap and straight across the top. Leave the castle over a bank, near a large holly

tree. Enter a field and bear left down and across field to gate, stile and F.P. sign. Turn left on road for 300 yards.

(9) Just before Star Cross, turn right on signed F.P. (Membury 3). Through gate and bear right across field towards gate in hedge opposite. Turn right at gate (do not go through gate) and follow hedge down to woods. Continue for 150 yards down to cattle trough. Cross a stile in corner and a wet area for a few yards and then fork left to walk on a bank (old field boundary) in plantation. Cross a stream (W.M. on tree) and continue uphill on same bank. Look for waymarks on trees and continue to a crossing track. Cross straight over (W.M. on tree) and climb steeply up through plantation (roughly follow near bank on left). Near the top, bear left to a stile. Over and up the right side of field to road and F.P. sign near house. (N.B. Path has now been diverted away from Twist Farm, as shown on O.S. map). Instead, now turn left on road to signed F.P. on right. Turn right (still on Membury 3) through gate and immediately right, through another gate (W.M.) and turn left to follow a hedge to gate (W.M.). Through and continue to corner.

(10) Turn right to next corner and through gate (end of diversion from OS map). In a few yards, turn left through gate on F.P. (Chardstock 23). Keep to right side of field to a small gate (W.M.). Through and immediately turn right over stile. Then turn left through long field.

(11) Towards end of field, fork right to gate in right corner. Go through into an old orchard and in a few yards, turn right on track. Follow along this, which continues as a F.P. coming in from a road below. Follow hedge on your right (Chardstock 34) to a gate in far top corner. Go through and ahead across middle of field to gate in far corner. Then proceed on the left of next field to gate and enclosed track (views to Membury Castle). Go down the track, leading to Yard Farm (avoid a left bend to a barn only). In 100 yards pass through the farmyard of Yard Farm.

(12) Follow farm road to junction with F.P. at right bend near a cottage. Turn left over a high stile onto enclosed F.P. (Chardstock 36, part of) and follow for 100 yards to gate. Through and turn right on F.P. (Chardstock 42). Follow track, with bracken covered slope on your

left and past a gate on your right. As boundary fence bends right continue ahead bearing to the right to join a B.W. coming from your left. Follow this down to gate onto lane at a bend. Proceed down the lane to a junction with a road and F.P. sign.

(13) Turn left on road. Go past the entrance drive to Churchill Farm. In 400 yards, turn right over stile on signed F.P. (Chardstock 41, part of). Keep down left side of field to a left bend in a hedge (a crossing hedge has been removed). Now cross field to right hand side and follow to the bottom corner and gate. Through and cross corner of field to gate near thatched farmhouse. Follow a track for 50 feet and cross the driveway of farm to gate. Now cross a small field to a small gate. Then down the right side of next field to a small gate. Follow down an enclosed track between a school and church to a road and F.P. sign. Turn left for a few yards back to village hall car park on right.

POINTS OF INTEREST

Membury village and castle: see walk 15

All Saints: this parish has been taken from Axminster parish. For a time it was in Dorset but was restored to Devon in 1896. It has a church, school, chapel, pub, post office, village hall and cricket ground; in effect a complete village.

Walk 17: Combe St Nicholas

WHITESTAUNTON • CINDER HILL • BEETHAM

Start: Lay-by on Taunton/Chard road, junction with Belcombe Drove
Map ref: ST 294120
Distance: 9 miles
Grading: Moderate
Refreshments: Provide your own
O.S. Maps: 1:50 000 Landranger- 193 (Taunton and Lyme Regis)
1:25 000 Pathfinder - ST21/31 (1278) Ilminster

DIRECTIONS

(1) Cross road from lay-by to gate opposite. Go through gate on F.P. (Combe St Nicholas CH7/26) and down left side of field. Pass through a gate on your left and continue in previous direction, but now with hedge on your right, through a second field. When hedgeline ends, follow a track to gate. Then cross a third field to a gate leading onto an enclosed track to road.

(2) Turn left and follow the road to Combe St Nicholas. Turn right through village to church and turn right again at the church. As this road bends right, turn left on a short F.P. between a bungalow and house. In 30 yards, turn left on road for 50 yards.

(3) Turn right down an enclosed track on signed F.P. (Combe St Nicholas CH7/2) signed to Brocole Lane in half a mile. Continue down this track and around a left bend. Through a gate at end of path into a field. Immediately turn left through another gate into field (W.M.). Then across a small corner of a field to a stile (W.M.). Over and uphill at left side of field to top. Through gate and go half left to gate in far corner. Now turn right on Brocole Lane (Combe St Nicholas CH7/4) to gate (W.M.). Enter field and head across to a stile opposite. Then follow at left side of next field to gate (W.M.). Keep to the left side of a third field, (with a bank sloping steeply away to the left). Continue to the corner of this field and turn right on another F.P. (Combe St Nicholas CH7/5) to the second gate on left (W.M.).

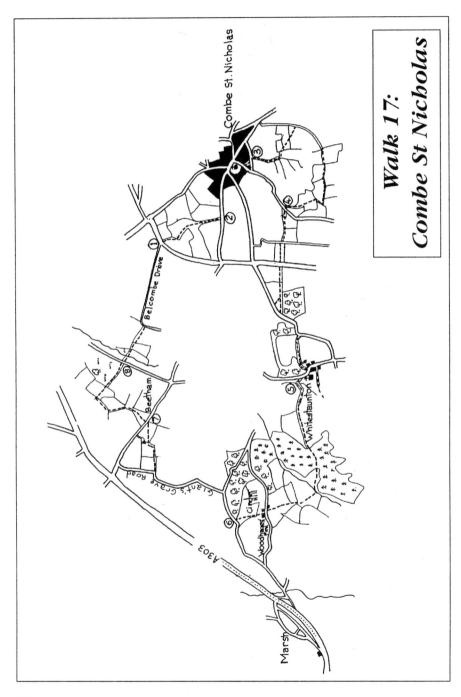

Walk 17:
Combe St Nicholas

Through and across middle of field to join the hedgeline to a gate and stile (W.M.). Keep forward on an enclosed track to a road. Cross over and up an enclosed and signed F.P. (Combe St Nicholas CH7/47). Enter a field and climb uphill for 50 yards to stile (W.M.). Over and up the right side of a second field to a gate and stile (W.M.). Turn left on a green lane and in a few yards, turn right through a small gate. Pass up through the middle of a field to a gate onto a road and cross over.

(4) Turn left to a stile on your right in 40 feet. Turn right over this and go straight ahead at the left edge of a very large field to a stile in bottom corner. Over and turn left on road. Just past a bungalow, as road bends to the left, continue straight ahead on an enclosed grass track (Whitestaunton CH29/1) called Courtfield Lane. Continue past farm buildings and follow to a road. Turn right through Whitestaunton and past the church for 50 yards.

(5) Turn left on signed F.P. (Whitestaunton CH29/6) signed to Cinder Hill. Follow this enclosed track to a gate and stile. Over and turn left with the track, by an old stone wall, to cross over a stream. Continue uphill, and bend right at the end of the stone wall to a gate and stile (W.M.). Follow an open track at the right side of a long field to a stile (W.M.). Enter a plantation and go straight ahead. Cross a forestry track and keep with F.P. for a short distance to join a hedgeline to a stile on your left. Over into a field and down half right through a steep field to a wire fence (W.M.). Then ahead to a F.B. Cross a stream and straight across field to a wide gap. Go through a gate (W.M.) to the right of the gap (removed hedge) and on uphill to hedge and gate near bend in hedgeline (W.M.). Through and up across field on B.W. (Whitestaunton 29/5, part of) to the left of farm buildings, at a road and B.W. sign. Cross straight over the road and through part of Woodhayes Farm yard on F.P. (Whitestaunton CH29/2). Go past a cottage on your left, to a gate near a chicken shed. Go through into field and follow a line of poles towards the left edge of some woods to a gate and out onto a road.

(6) Turn right on road and follow for 400 yards. Bear left at a road junction. Follow along Giant Grave road for a further 800 yards to a left bend. Turn right over a stile, beside a gate (N.B. avoid the first

signed F.P. along this road) on F.P. (Combe St Nicholas CH7/48, part of). Walk down right side of field to stile in corner. Over, and bend left with hedgeline at far end of field to gate, 50 yards short of a small barn. Through and across field to gate onto road and turn right.

(7) In about 100 yards turn left up some steep steps in a wall on a signed F.P. (Combe St Nicholas CH7/32, part of). (N.B. The F.P. sign is in the field at top of steps). Climb over a stile and cross field at right edge. As hedge turns right bear left across field to gate in corner. Through gateway and head up the left side of field. Pass through a gateway. Then turn right to follow hedge to gate. Turn right and down across field to gate. Now cross a rough and reedy pasture (Fresh Moor) to a small gate. Continue down right side of field to stile, road and F.P. sign. Cross straight over road on diversion of F.P. (Combe St Nicholas CH7/33) to gate opposite. Then down across field and cross over a stream. Proceed up the left side of field to gate and stile. Over and follow left side of second field to gateway. Turn left on wide grass track (Combe St Nicholas CH7/46). Turn right in 50 yards on Belcombe Drove. Follow this for half a mile to road and lay-by parking.

POINTS OF INTEREST

Whitestaunton: the manor house has an old Roman villa within its grounds, discovered in 1882 by the owners.

Horsepool Copse, nearby, contains a prehistoric earthwork known as Whitestaunton Camp.

St Andrew's church was built between 1483 and 1492. Two of the five bells are pre-reformation.

Walk 18: Blackborough

BLACKBOROUGH COMMON • FOREST GLADE •
KNOWLES WOOD • HILL GATE • SAINT HILL •
HOLLIS GREEN • BLACKBOROUGH HOUSE

Start: Roadside, near site of former Blackborough church (now demolished)
Map ref: ST094092
Distance: 6½ miles
Grading: Easy to moderate (one steep climb to start)
Refreshments: Provide your own
O.S. Maps: 1:50 000 Landranger - 192 Exeter and Sidmouth
1:25 000 Pathfinder - ST00/10 (1296) Honiton and Cullompton

DIRECTIONS

(1) Cross the road from site of Blackborough Church to signed F.P. (Kentisbeare 18) at side of house. Climb steeply up an enclosed track to a crossing track. Turn right on signed F.P. (Kentisbeare 19) and follow past a trig point. Path then bears left and continues with conifers on the left and mixed woodland on the right. In half a mile, turn left at junction on signed track. Turn right at the next T junction and through a gate and ahead to a road and F.P. sign.

(2) Turn left and then right at the next gate into a plantation (not into field). Squeeze between this gate and a post (N.B. this is a permissive path and not a public footpath) and fork right on a clear track at edge of plantation. After 400 yards, path descends to a five way junction of paths. Fork left on signed F.P. (Kentisbeare 40) and continue to junction of paths and a waymark post. Turn right and in 20 yards, turn left on a waymarked F.P. In a further 50 yards, turn right (W.M.'d) and immediately left (W.M.'d) to walk in previous direction. Follow a bank in the plantation to a crossing track.

(3) Go straight over, now at the left side of a field used for camping. On reaching the far corner, cross over track (leading to caravan site). In 30-40 yards turn right on waymarked F.P. (Kentisbeare 40). Continue on forest track and over two crossing tracks. Towards the

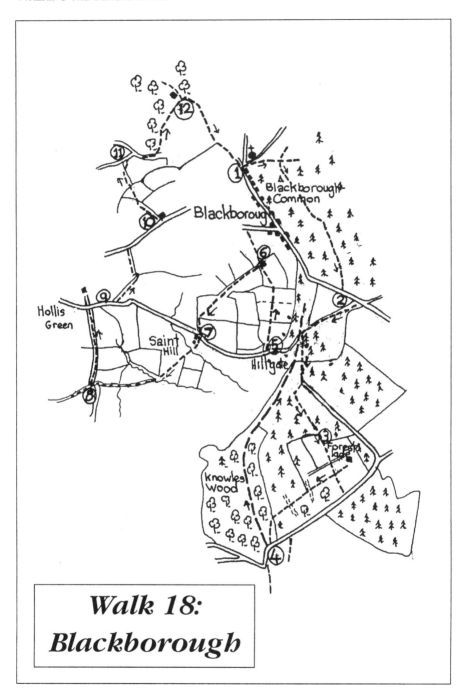

Walk 18:
Blackborough

end of the path, it bends left between rhododendron bushes, forming an arch. Follow the track downhill to near a road.

(4) Turn right on signed B.W. (Kentisbeare 41). Keep on this path for nearly a mile to a five way junction of paths (N.B. this is the same junction as you reached in paragraph (2)). Turn back sharp left at this point and downhill past a new house on a bend. Continue for 200 yards to a seat and F.P. sign (Kentisbeare 21).

(5) Turn right on an enclosed track to a gate and stile in 80 yards. Over and across field to gap in hedge. Now cross a second field to a gap in line of old hedge (some trees remaining). Cross a third field to a gate (W.M.). Through and bear left across fourth field to a gate near a white cottage. Go through and past the cottage to a gate on your left (W.M.) just before barn.

(6) Turn left through gate on waymarked F.P. (Kentisbeare 23). Continue downhill at the right edge of a field to a gate at the end. Now follow a clear track, with a small wood on your left, to a gate in 100 yards. Enter a field and follow the hedge until reaching a concrete water trough in 35 yards. Then, as the hedge bends right, bear left across field to gate. Through and along right side of field to a gate onto road at Saint Hill and a F.P. sign.

(7) Follow the road past a chapel and when it bears left, continue straight ahead on a track which is a signed F.P. (Kentisbeare 28). Go past a cottage on right for 150 yards and cross over a stream. Proceed on a hedged track for a further 40 yards to a gate (W.M.). Enter a field and fork right across field (30° from hedge) to a gate and waymark. Through gate and across a stream. Then turn right at F.P. sign to a gate in 50 yards (across the track). Pass through a farm and over a stream. Follow the farm road uphill to just past a red brick house.

(8) Turn right on track as F.P. (Kentisbeare 11). Follow this farm track down to a road. Turn right, and pass by Hollis Green Cottage on the right.

(9) Just past cottages on the left, climb over a stile on F.P. (Kentisbeare 25). Follow up the left side of one field to a gate on left (W.M.). Through and immediately over a stile on left (W.M.) and turn right along hedgeline on F.P. (Kentisbeare 24, part of) to stile in corner and

F.P. sign. Turn right on road to Poole House on your right.

(10) Turn left on signed F.P. (Kentisbeare 26) at side of farm buildings. Through a gate and ahead at right side of field to gate on right (W.M.). Through and bear left across field to F.B., 30 yards from corner of field. Over and bear right to far corner of field to gate (W.M.).

(11) Through and turn right on F.P. (Kentisbeare 35) along a track for 30 yards to a stile (W.M.). Over and continue on grass track which enters a field. Bear left to follow up left side of field by woods, on a sunken path to gate by Blackborough House and F.P. sign.

(12) Turn right on drive and follow this back to Blackborough churchyard.

POINTS OF INTEREST

Until the late 1930s, Blackborough was a centre for whetstone quarrying. The women used to shape the stones that their menfolk had quarried. These stones were taken to Exeter or Taunton markets in pannier bags on donkeys. They came back with river mud to put on their gardens.

Blackborough church has recently been demolished because of bad building construction. It was built about 170 years ago by Lord Egremont who then lived at Blackborough House. The grounds of the old house are now used as a car breakers' yard.

Walk 19: Luppitt

HENSE MOOR • MATHAYES FARM • HILLEND FARM •
WHIPPINS COTTAGE • MOHUNS OTTERY •
BEACON • GOULDS FARM

Start: Luppitt village hall
Map ref: ST170065
Map ref: ST180068 (Point 10 on map) if wishing to divide walk into
two parts.
Distance: 6½ miles
Grading: Moderate, very wet in places especially over Hense Moor
Refreshments: Provide your own
O.S. Maps: 1:50 000 Landranger - 193 (Taunton and Lyme Regis)
1:25 000 Pathfinder - ST00/10 (1296) Honiton and Cullompton

DIRECTIONS

(1) From village hall turn left down road to signed F.P. on left (Luppitt
No. 14). Through gate and straight across field to stile and F.B.
opposite. Over and turn left on surfaced track to Brook Cottage. Turn
right on signed F.P. Go past a wooden bungalow and follow a clear but
very wet track, which runs into another track from the left. Continue
ahead through bracken on clear path to a metalled crossing track.
Cross straight over and follow track to a stile. Over and bear left across
field to stile.

(2) Climb over stile and bear right on track between bracken, gorse and
brambles which gradually descends. The path finally descends more
steeply through a very wet and boggy area down to a small gate and
F.B. Cross stream and bear left up the right side of some very wet
woods to a cottage.

(3) Turn left on the cottage drive. In 20 yards, turn right at F.P. sign
(still Luppitt 14) through bracken and brambles. The path continues
at the side of a wire fence. At a point where this bends left uphill, and
the hedge on your right bears to the right, continue ahead and slightly
down across an area of bracken and tussocks of grass. Follow roughly a
line of overhead cables between bushes, down to a F.B. Cross this and

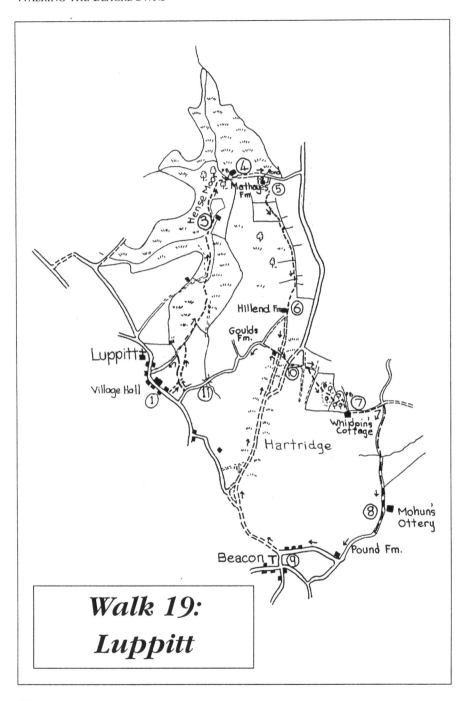

Walk 19: Luppitt

turn right on a very wet path between trees in woods. In 50 yards bear left to follow a minor stream in the direction of Turf House.

(4) Turn right on the drive of Turf House (F.P. Luppitt No. 17) and follow this to a point about level with Mathayes Farm (about 100 yards away to your right). Turn right here through nettles to a fence. Climb over and follow around a man made pond and over a F.B. Follow path towards the farmhouse to a gate.

(5) The path now continues between the farmhouse and a building used as a brewery. Just past the brewery (you can go no further) turn right through door and go through the brewery itself and out into a small garden area to a stile. (N.B. There is a legal right of way through the brewery. There will probably be a diversion from point 4 at some later date. This will be signed). Climb over this stile and follow a track uphill to a gate. Through and bear left up to the top corner of field. Go through a gate and follow along a ridge, through two fields to a gate and stile. Now pass through a horse training area and a small paddock to a gate. Follow a track in the next field, which drops down to a stile and gate at Hillend Farm. Go through the farmyard to a road and F.P. sign.

(6) Go straight ahead on an unfenced road to a crossing public F.P.

(10) Turn left and climb steeply uphill on signed F.P. (Luppitt No. 26, part of) N.B. there is a seat at the top making this a good lunch stop with panoramic views. (If wishing to do this walk in two parts then this is the alternative parking place on road verge).

From the seat cross over a road and F.P. opposite, over a stile onto an enclosed track. Follow this to a crossing track. Go over this and bear right on signed F.P. across a field between wire fencing to another crossing track. Turn left and immediately right on signed F.P. through a gate. Bear right across a field to a waymarked gate on fence. Proceed down through a new deciduous plantation and pass to the right of a pond. Continue on clear path to a stile and waymark giving access into a piece of wet woodland. Bear left across this avoiding a private wood and nature reserve on your right. On reaching a ditch, cross a F.B. and turn right on a bank. Follow this bank and turn left past some fencing erected to screen Whippins Cottage.

(7) Come out onto a clear unfenced track (drive to Cottage). Follow this down to a left bend in 300 yards. Go straight ahead into a field. Turn right on a B.W. (Luppitt No. 25) along the right side of field. Pass through gateways and ahead to another gate. Now follow an enclosed farm track past Mohuns Ottery Farm onto entrance gates at end of farm drive.

(8) Turn right with the road. At the next junction, turn right at Pound Farm and follow uphill for 400 yards. Go past some pretty cottages to a junction by a telephone box.

(9) Turn right and follow this unfenced road for one mile, below Hartridge Hill. This road is fairly level, but when it starts to climb steeply uphill at a road sign (signed to Luppitt and Upottery) take the left fork, signed to Luppitt.

(10) Continue to a crossing F.P. (Luppitt 26 again) and turn left on this signed F.P. (This is the point at which you turned right previously in this figure of eight walk up to a seat). Follow down across common to join a farm track. In 50 yards, join a lane coming in from the right. Follow this around a left bend and past Goulds Farm. Proceed past a second farm to road bridge.

(11) Continue on road to a T junction and turn right back to Luppitt village hall car park.

POINTS OF INTEREST

Luppitt village is mentioned in Domesday Book, along with Shopscombe, Greenway Farm and Mohuns Ottery.

The village, like others in the Blackdowns, was famous for the smuggling of brandy during the 18th century.

At the entrance to the church car park is the Luppitt Stone, embedded in the hedge by the cattle grid. Stones like this can be found in other villages and are called 'devil' stones. The one in Luppitt was used in 1550 to unload the tenor bell.

The 13th century church of St Mary the Virgin is very large for the size of the village and has a waggon roof made from local wood.

Walk 20: Dalwood
(FIGURE OF EIGHT WALK - 9 MILES)

PART 1 (6 MILES): DANES HILL CROSS • BECKFORD BRIDGE • RIVER YARTY • HIGHER WESTWATER FARM • OLD CORYTON FARM • FORDHAYES FARM • CLIFTHORNE FARM • NOWER FARM • NAISHES LANE

PART 2 (3 MILES): DALWOOD PRIMARY SCHOOL • HAWLEY BOTTOM • HAWLEY CROSS • COMBEHEAD FARM • PARISH BOUNDARY TO HAM ROAD • DALWOOD

Start: (Part 1) - The Tuckers Arms, Dalwood
Map ref: ST249005
Distance: Total of 9 miles (6 + 3)
Grading: Part 1 - Moderate/easy; Part 2 - Easy
Refreshments: The Tuckers Arms Inn
O.S. Maps: 1:50 000 Landranger - 193 (Taunton and Lyme Regis)
1:25 000 Pathfinder - ST20/30 (1297) Chard

DIRECTIONS: PART 1 – 6 MILES

(1) Turn right from Tuckers Arms (or left from village car park) and follow road over Corry Brook in 100 yards. Continue to a left bend (by telephone box) and proceed straight ahead on signed F.P. (Dalwood 23). Follow a concrete drive to cottage. Then through W.M.'d gate on left (to follow diversion around cottage) and turn right to follow hedge to gate (W.M.'d). Through and ahead up and across field to stile. Cross corner of next field to gateway. Through and along the left edge of third field to a stile. Now continue up the side of a garden hedge, through a rough area of brambles and nettles, climbing steeply to join the concreted drive of a cottage. Follow this up to a road and F.P. sign.

(2) Turn left on road to Danes Hill cross roads. Turn right on Dalwood Lane that ends at a white cottage. Proceed past this on a grass lane for 40 yards to a gate and F.P. sign on the left. Turn through this gate on F.P. (Dalwood 25) and descend through middle of field to stile in left hedge, 100 yards from corner. Cross over and down the middle of next field to a gate and F.P. sign on right at the bottom of the field.

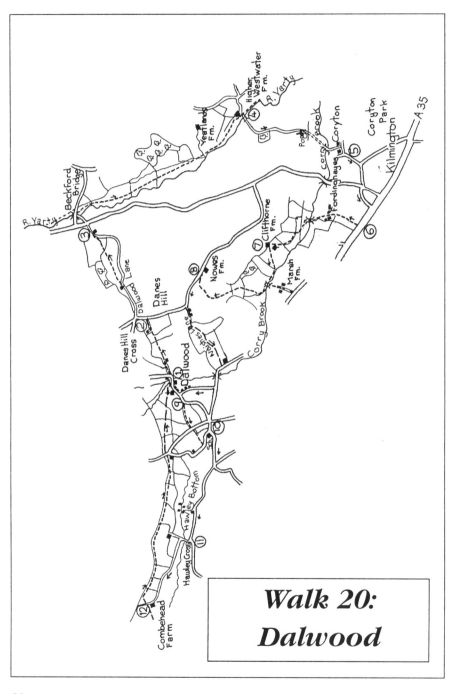

Walk 20:
Dalwood

Turn left down a short enclosed track to a road and F.P. sign at a road junction.

(3) Cross straight over and down road opposite to Beckford Bridge. Here, cross the River Yarty by the road bridge (ford) or the old packhorse bridge nearby. Turn right on signed F.P. (Membury 10, part of) and cross field by the river to a F.B. over a side stream. The F.P. now crosses into Axminster parish and continues as (Axminster 42) across a second field to a gate and a third field to a small gate. Cross the middle of fourth field to a gap in a barbed wire fence. Then bear left to field bridge and across fifth field on a track to a gate in 50 yards. Through and cross sixth field (Yarty Farm away on your left) to a gate and stile. Cross seventh field to right of a thatched farmhouse (Higher Westwater Farm) and F.P. sign. Go out onto farm road.

(4) Turn right and cross River Yarty by F.B. and continue on enclosed track for about half a mile to pond on right and gate ahead. Through gate and cross field on an open track to F.B. Cross over Corry Brook and ahead through Old Coryton Farm. Turn right on farm road to junction with council road and F.P. sign.

(5) Turn left (signed Kilmington and Axminster). At a left bend in road, go straight ahead at junction (6' 6" width sign). Go past a right junction and track to left. Continue to junction with A35. Turn right on this busy road (walk on verge) for 250 yards to signed F.P. and drive to Fordhayes Farm.

(6) Turn right down drive on F.P. (Kilmington 9) to barn conversions. Go between these cottages on a gravelled drive. Go through entrance drive of bottom cottage on left and down (W.M.'d) F.P. by a wire fence to a stile. Then bear left down across a field to a F.B. over Corry Brook. Cross F.B. and bear left across field to a double stile in hedge opposite. Cross next field to a gate opposite, in corner of another field. Pass through and turn left along hedge to gate. Through and bear right up towards barn and Clifthorne Farm.

(7) Turn left before barn and bear left and down across field on F.P. (Kilmington 8, part of) to gate in bottom corner. Through and across field to gate. Ahead to F.B., over Corry Brook. Do not cross F.B., but leave field on F.P. (Kilmington 11, part of) through a gate. Turn right

on track for a few yards to gate. Through and follow hedge to a gate on right. Through and bear left across next field to a F.B. Then bear left across field to gate. Through and straight up and across next field to gate at top. Now follow an open track, climbing steeply up to a gate. Through and bear right up farm track to road at Nower Farm.

(8) Turn left on road and on to a B.W. sign on left. Turn back left on this B.W. (Dalwood 28) and past two cottages (Rutland and Green View). At bottom of lane, bear right down a waymarked enclosed track for 200 yards to a small gate. Go through and B.W. continues down the right side of field to another small gate. Now continue at the left side of field to third small gate, in a corner and ahead to fourth small gate. The track is now enclosed again until a gate. Follow down a concreted drive for 50 feet to road and F.P. sign. Turn right and follow over road bridge. Turn right at next junction and on to crossroads. Turn right to a T junction at Dalwood.

(9) Turn right down to Tuckers Arms for lunch or a picnic by Corry Brook.

DIRECTIONS: PART 2 – 3 MILES

(1) Turn left from Tuckers Arms car park. Go past the church and a left junction.

(9) Continue to a left bend in road. Then go straight ahead on unsigned F.P. (Dalwood 15) between two bungalows. Pass a set of garages to a kissing gate. Then keep at the right side of field to gate and road. Cross straight over on signed F.P. (still Dalwood 15) and along left edge of field to end of hedge. Bear left across remainder of field to gate onto road. Turn left to a T junction at school.

(10) Turn right and uphill to junction on right (signed to Hawley Bottom). Follow road past a F.P. sign at Hawley Bottom. Continue on the road for a further 600 yards to Hawley Cross and fork right on a 'No through road'.

(11) Bear right with this lane to a signed B.W. on left, opposite Hawley Cottage. Turn left on this enclosed B.W. (Dalwood 35). Go past two cottages on your left. Turn right at T junction on a stony track past Combehead Farm. Arrive at a crossing F.P. sign.

(12) Turn right up steps and over a stile on F.P. (Dalwood 6), to join and follow hedgeline through eight fields on the parish boundary. The last field is a horse paddock for stables. Pass to the left of this to a road, F.P. and B.W. signs.

(13) Cross over road on signed F.P. (Dalwood 2). Go through a small gate and down left edge of field to gateway. Through and fork right across field to gate, stile and waymark. Cross a third field to a F.B. and a fourth field to a gate at the left of Dalwood church. Go down a path to emerge at the village hall car park. Turn right and immediately left between car park on your left and a cottage. Follow F.P. out onto road in Dalwood. Turn right back to the Tuckers Arms.

POINTS OF INTEREST

Dalwood is an attractive village on the edge of the Blackdown Hills, three miles from Axminster. It lies in the valley of the Corry Brook. Until 1842 Dalwood was in Dorset. The right to hold an annual fair was granted in 1343 by Edward III. This has now been re-established, after a lapse in the 19th century. It is a jolly event and is held in August.

The church of St Peter was built in the 15th century and the Tuckers Arms was built to house the men building the church.

Nearby at Loughwood is a little Baptist Chapel built in the 17th century and now in the hands of the National Trust. It has been re-thatched and restored. The original pulpit, box pews and baptistry remain. It was once used by dissenters who could easily escape into nearby Devon or Dorset.